AN OUTLINE OF
Psychoanalysis

By Sigmund Freud

AN OUTLINE OF
Psychoanalysis

❧ ❧

SIGMUND FREUD

❧ ❧

Authorized translation by JAMES STRACHEY

W · W · NORTON & COMPANY · INC ·

NEW YORK

First published in German
under the title of
ABRISS DER PSYCHO-ANALYSE
1940

W. W. Norton & Company, Inc. is also the publisher
of the works of Erik H. Erikson, Otto Fenichel, Karen Horney and
Harry Stack Sullivan, and the principal works of Sigmund Freud.

PRINTED IN THE UNITED STATES OF AMERICA

23456789

Contents

CONTENTS

Translator's Preface

FREUD began writing this unfinished *Abriss der Psycho-analyse*—his last work of any considerable length—in London on July 22, 1938. A few weeks later he broke it off at a point where, to all appearances, it cannot have been very far from completion. He never returned to it, but, in the following October, started upon a similar project, to which he gave an English title, *Some Elementary Lessons in Psycho-Analysis*. This second version, however, included in Vol. V of Freud's *Collected Papers*, extends to only a few pages.

The present *Outline* was first published in German in the *Internationale Zeitschrift für Psychoanalyse und Imago*, XXV (1940), and is included in Vol. XVII of Freud's *Gesammelte Werke*. An English translation appeared in the *International Journal of Psycho-Analysis*, XXI (1940), and is now reprinted with considerable revisions.

The third chapter, unlike the rest of the book, was noted down by the author in a series of abbreviated jottings in telegraphic style. These are, however, perfectly clear and consecutive, and it has been easy for the editors of the German edition to expand them, without any other alteration, into complete sentences. Part One bears no title in the original manuscript and one has been supplied by me.

I have to thank Miss Anna Freud for much valuable help.

J. S.

Introductory Note

THE AIM of this brief work is to bring together the doctrines of psychoanalysis and to state them, as it were, dogmatically—in the most concise form and in the most positive terms. Its intention is naturally not to compel belief or to establish conviction.

The teachings of psychoanalysis are based upon an incalculable number of observations and experiences, and no one who has not repeated those observations upon himself or upon others is in a position to arrive at an independent judgment of it.

PART ONE

The Mind and
Its Workings

CHAPTER ONE

The Psychical Apparatus

⋞⧽⧼⋟
⋞⧽⧼⋟

PSYCHOANALYSIS makes a basic assumption,[1] the discussion of which falls within the sphere of philosophical thought, but the justification of which lies in its results. We know two things concerning what we call our psyche or mental life: firstly, its bodily organ and scene of action, the brain (or nervous system), and secondly, our acts of consciousness, which are immediate data and cannot be more fully explained by any kind of description. Everything that lies between these two terminal points is unknown to us and, so far as we are aware, there is no direct relation between them. If

[1] [It will be seen that this basic assumption is a double-barrelled one and is sometimes referred to by the author as two separate hypotheses. So, for instance, in the next paragraph, and on pages 34–35; but again as a single one on page 105.—Trans.]

it existed, it would at the most afford an exact localization of the processes of consciousness and would give us no help toward understanding them.

Our two hypotheses start out from these ends or beginnings of our knowledge. The first is concerned with localization. We assume that mental life is the function of an apparatus to which we ascribe the characteristics of being extended in space and of being made up of several portions—which we imagine, that is, as being like a telescope or microscope or something of the sort. The consistent carrying through of a conception of this kind is a scientific novelty, even though some attempts in that direction have been made previously.

We have arrived at our knowledge of this psychical apparatus by studying the individual development of human beings. To the oldest of these mental provinces or agencies we give the name of *id*. It contains everything that is inherited, that is present at birth, that is fixed in the constitution—above all, therefore, the instincts, which originate in the somatic organization and which find their first mental expression in the id in forms unknown to us.[2]

---

[2] This oldest portion of the mental apparatus remains the most important throughout life, and it was the first subject of the investigations of psychoanalysis. [Throughout this book the English word "instinct" is, with some misgivings, used to render the German "*Trieb*." The sense in which Freud uses the term is, in any case, made clear in the following pages.—*Trans.*]

Under the influence of the real external world which surrounds us, one portion of the id has undergone a special development. From what was originally a cortical layer, provided with organs for receiving stimuli and with apparatus for protection against excessive stimulation, a special organization has arisen which henceforward acts as an intermediary between the id and the external world. This region of our mental life has been given the name of *ego*.

The principal characteristics of the ego are these. In consequence of the relation which was already established between sensory perception and muscular action, the ego is in control of voluntary movement. It has the task of self-preservation. As regards *external* events, it performs that task by becoming aware of the stimuli from without, by storing up experiences of them (in the memory), by avoiding excessive stimuli (through flight), by dealing with moderate stimuli (through adaptation) and, finally, by learning to bring about appropriate modifications in the external world to its own advantage (through activity). As regards *internal* events, in relation to the id, it performs that task by gaining control over the demands of the instincts, by deciding whether they shall be allowed to obtain satisfaction, by postponing that satisfaction to times and circumstances favorable in the external world or by suppressing their excitations completely. Its activities are governed by consideration of the tensions produced by stimuli present within it or introduced into it. The raising of these tensions is in general felt as *unpleasure* and their lowering as *pleasure*. It is probable, however, that what is felt as pleasure or unpleasure is not the *absolute* degree of the tensions but something in the rhythm of their changes. The ego pursues pleasure and seeks to avoid unpleasure. An increase in unpleasure which is expected and foreseen is met by a *signal of anxiety*; the occasion of this increase, whether it threatens from without or within, is called a *danger*. From time to time the ego gives up its connection with the external world and withdraws into the state of sleep, in which its organization undergoes far-reaching changes. It may be inferred from the state of sleep that that organization consists in a particular distribution of mental energy.

The long period of childhood, during which the growing human being lives in dependence upon his parents, leaves behind it a precipitate, which forms within his ego a special agency in which this parental influence is prolonged. It has received the name of *superego*. In so far as the superego is differentiated from the ego or opposed to it, it constitutes a third force which the ego must take into account.

Thus, an action by the ego is as it should be if it satisfies simultaneously the demands of the id, of the super-ego and of reality, that is to say if it is able to reconcile their demands with one another. The details of the relation between the ego and the superego become completely intelligible if they are carried back to the child's attitude toward his parents. The parents' influence naturally includes not merely the personalities of the parents themselves but also the racial, national, and family traditions handed on through them as well as the demands of the immediate social *milieu* which they represent. In the same way, an individual's superego in the course of his development takes over contributions from later successors and substitutes of his parents, such as teachers, admired figures in public life, or high social ideals. It will be seen that, in spite of their fundamental difference, the id and the superego have one thing in common: they both represent the influences of the past (the id the influence of heredity, the superego essentially the influence of what is taken over from other people), whereas the ego is principally determined by the individual's own experience, that is to say by accidental and current events.

This general pattern of a psychical apparatus may be supposed to apply equally to the higher animals which resemble man mentally. A superego must be presumed to be present wherever, as in the case of man, there is a long period of dependence in childhood. The assumption of a distinction between ego and id cannot be avoided.

Animal psychology has not yet taken in hand the interesting problem which is here presented.

CHAPTER TWO

The Theory of the Instincts

৺ই ই৵

৺ই ই৵

THE POWER of the id expresses the true purpose of the individual organism's life. This consists in the satisfaction of its innate needs. No such purpose as that of keeping itself alive or of protecting itself from dangers by means of anxiety can be attributed to the id. That is the business of the ego, which is also concerned with discovering the most favorable and least perilous method of obtaining satisfaction, taking the external world into account. The superego may bring fresh needs to the fore, but its chief function remains the *limitation* of satisfactions.

The forces which we assume to exist behind the tensions caused by the needs of the id are called *instincts*. They represent the somatic demands upon mental life. Though they are the ultimate cause of all activity, they are by nature conservative; the state, whatever it may be, which a living thing has reached, gives rise to a tendency to re-establish that state so soon as it has been abandoned. It is possible to distinguish an indeterminate number of instincts and in common practice this is in fact done. For us, however, the important question arises whether we may not be able to derive all of these various instincts from a few fundamental ones. We have found that instincts can change their aim (by displacement) and also that they can replace one another—the energy of one instinct passing over to another. This latter process is still insufficiently understood. After long doubts and vacillations we have decided to assume the existence of only two basic instincts, *Eros* and *the destructive instinct*. (The contrast between the instincts of self-preservation and of the preservation of the species, as well as the contrast between ego-love and object-love, fall within the bounds of Eros.) The aim of the first of these basic instincts is to establish ever greater unities and to preserve them thus—in short, to bind together; the aim of the second, on the contrary, is to undo connections and so to destroy things. We may suppose that the final aim of the destructive instinct 's to reduce living things to an inorganic state. For this reason we also call it the *death instinct*. If we suppose that living things appeared later than inanimate ones and arose out of them, then the death instinct agrees with the formula that we have stated, to the effect that instincts tend toward a return to an earlier state. We are unable to apply the formula to Eros (the love instinct). That would be to imply that living substance had once been a unity but had subsequently been torn apart and was now tending toward re-union.[3]

In biological functions the two basic instincts work against each other or combine with each other. Thus, the act of eating is a destruction of the object with the final aim of incorporating it, and the sexual act is an act of aggression having as its purpose the most intimate union. This interaction of the two basic instincts with and against each other gives rise to the whole variegation of the phenomena of life. The analogy of our two basic instincts extends from the region of animate things to the pair of opposing forces—attraction and repulsion—which rule in the inorganic world.[4]

Modifications in the proportions of the fusion between the instincts have the most noticeable results. A surplus of sexual aggressiveness will change a lover into a sexual murderer, while a sharp diminution in the aggressive factor will lead to shyness or impotence.

There can be no question of restricting one or the

---

[3] Something of the sort has been imagined by poets, but nothing like it is known to us from the actual history of living substance.

[4] This picture of the basic forces or instincts, which still arouses much opposition among analysts, was already a familiar one to the philosopher Empedocles of Acragas.

other of the basic instincts to a single region of the mind. They are necessarily present everywhere. We may picture an initial state of things by supposing that the whole available energy of Eros, to which we shall henceforward give the name of *libido*, is present in the as yet undifferentiated ego-id and serves to neutralize the destructive impulses which are simultaneously present. (There is no term analogous to "libido" for describing the energy of the destructive instinct.) It becomes relatively easy for us to follow the later vicissitudes of the libido; but this is more difficult with the destructive instinct.

So long as that instinct operates internally, as a death instinct, it remains silent; we only come across it after it has become diverted outward as an instinct of destruction. That that diversion should occur seems essential for the preservation of the individual; the musculature is employed for the purpose. When the super-ego begins to be formed, considerable amounts of the aggressive instinct become fixated within the ego and operate there in a self-destructive fashion. This is one of the dangers to health to which mankind become subject on the path to cultural development. The holding back of aggressiveness is in general unhealthy and leads to illness. A person in a fit of rage often demonstrates how the transition from restrained aggressiveness to self-destructiveness is effected, by turning his aggressiveness against himself: he tears his hair or beats his face with his fists—treatment which he would evidently have preferred to apply to someone else. Some portion of self-destructiveness remains permanently within, until it at length succeeds in doing the individual to death, not, perhaps, until his libido has been used up or has become fixated in some disadvantageous way. Thus it may in general be suspected that the *individual* dies of his internal conflicts but that the *species* dies of its unsuccessful struggle against the external world, when the latter undergoes changes of a kind that cannot be dealt with by the adaptations which the species has acquired.

It is difficult to say anything of the behavior of the libido in the id and in the superego. Everything that we know about it relates to the ego, in which the whole available amount of libido is at first stored up. We call this state of things absolute, primary *narcissism*. It continues until the ego begins to cathect [5] the presentations of objects with libido—to change narcissistic libido into *object libido*. Throughout life the ego remains the great reservoir from which libidinal cathexes [5] are sent out on to objects and into which they are also once

---

[5] [The words "cathexis" and "to cathect" are used as renderings of the German "*Besetzung*" and "*besetzen*." These are the terms with which Freud expresses the idea of psychical energy being lodged in or attaching itself to mental structures or processes, somewhat on the analogy of an electric charge.—*Trans.*]

more withdrawn, like the pseudopodia of a body of protoplasm. It is only when someone is completely in love that the main quantity of libido is transferred on to the object and the object to some extent takes the place of the ego. A characteristic of libido which is important in life is its *mobility*, the ease with which it passes from one object to another. This must be contrasted with the *fixation* of libido to particular objects, which often persists through life.

There can be no question that the libido has somatic sources, that it streams into the ego from various organs and parts of the body. This is most clearly seen in the case of the portion of the libido which, from its instinctual aim, is known as sexual excitation. The most prominent of the parts of the body from which this libido arises are described by the name of *erotogenic zones*, though strictly speaking the whole body is an erotogenic zone. The greater part of what we know about Eros—that is, about its exponent, the libido—has been gained from the study of the sexual function, which, indeed, in the popular view, if not in our theory, coincides with Eros. We have been able to form a picture of the way in which the sexual impulse, which is destined to exercise a decisive influence on our life, gradually develops out of successive contributions from a number of component instincts, which represent particular erotogenic zones.

CHAPTER THREE

The Development of the Sexual Function

ACCORDING to the popular view, human sexual life consists essentially in the impulse to bring one's own genitals into contact with those of someone of the opposite sex. With this are associated, as accessory phenomena and introductory acts, kissing this extraneous body, looking at and touching it. This impulse is supposed to make its appearance at puberty, that is, at the age of sexual maturity, and to serve the purposes of reproduction. Nevertheless, certain facts have always been known that fail to fit into the narrow framework of this view. (1) It is a remarkable fact that there are people who are only attracted by the persons and genitals of members of their own sex. (2) It is equally remarkable that there are people whose desires behave in every way like sexual ones, but who at the same time entirely disregard the sexual organs or their normal use; people of this kind are known as "perverts." (3) And finally it is striking that many children (who are on that account regarded as degenerates) take a very early interest in their genitals and show signs of excitation in them.

It may well be believed that psychoanalysis provoked astonishment and denials when, partly upon the basis of these three neglected facts, it contradicted all the popular opinions upon sexuality. Its principal findings are as follows:

(*a*) Sexual life does not begin only at puberty, but starts with clear manifestations soon after birth.

(*b*) It is necessary to distinguish sharply between the concepts of "sexual" and "genital." The former is the wider concept and includes many activities that have nothing to do with the genitals.

(*c*) Sexual life comprises the function of obtaining pleasure from zones of the body—a function which is subsequently brought into the service of that of reproduction. The two functions often fail to coincide completely.

The chief interest is naturally focused upon the first

of these assertions, the most unexpected of all. It has been found that in early childhood there are signs of bodily activity to which only ancient prejudice could deny the name of sexual, and which are connected with mental phenomena that we come across later in adult love, such as fixation to a particular object, jealousy, and so on. It is further found that these phenomena which emerge in early childhood form part of a regular process of development, that they undergo a steady increase and reach a climax toward the end of the fifth year, after which there follows a lull. During this lull, progress is at a standstill and much is unlearned and undone. After the end of this period of latency, as it is called, sexual life is resumed with puberty, or, as we might say, it has a second efflorescence. Here we come upon the fact that the onset of sexual life is *diphasic*, that it occurs in two waves; this is unknown except in man and evidently has an important bearing upon his genesis.[6] It is not a matter of indifference that, with few exceptions, the events of the early period of sexuality fall a victim

---

[6] Cf. the hypothesis that man is descended from a mammal which reached sexual maturity at the age of five, but that some great external influence was brought to bear upon the species and interrupted the straight line of development of sexuality. This may also have been related to some other transformations in the sexual life of man as compared with that of animals, such as the suppression of the periodicity of the libido and the exploitation of the part played by menstruation in the relation between the sexes.

to *infantile amnesia*. Our understanding of the etiology of the neuroses and the technique of analytic therapy are derived from these views; and the tracing of the process of development in this early period has also provided evidence for yet other conclusions.

The first organ to make its appearance as an erotogenic zone and to make libidinal demands upon the mind is, from the time of birth onward, the mouth. To begin with, all mental activity is centered upon the task of providing satisfaction for the needs of that zone. In the first instance, of course, the latter serves the purposes of self-preservation by means of nourishment; but physiology should not be confused with psychology. The baby's obstinate persistence in sucking gives evidence at an early stage of a need for satisfaction which, although it originates from and is stimulated by the taking of nourishment, nevertheless seeks to obtain pleasure independently of nourishment and for that reason may and should be described as "sexual."

Sadistic impulses already begin to occur sporadically during the oral phase along with the appearance of the teeth. Their extent increases greatly during the second phase, which we describe as the sadistic-anal phase, because satisfaction is then sought in aggression and in the excretory function. We justify our inclusion of aggressive impulses in the libido by supposing that sadism is an instinctual fusion of purely libidinal and purely destructive impulses, a fusion which thenceforward persists without interruption.[7]

The third phase is the so-called phallic one, which is, as it were, a forerunner of the final shape of sexual life, and already greatly resembles it. It is to be noted that what comes in question at this stage is not the genitals of both sexes but only those of the male (the phallus). The female genitals long remain unknown: in the child's attempt at understanding sexual processes, he pays homage to the venerable cloacal theory—a theory which has a genetic justification.[8]

With the phallic phase and in the course of it the sexuality of early childhood reaches its height and approaches its decline. Thenceforward boys and girls have different histories. To begin with, both place their intellectual activity at the service of sexual research; both start off from the presumption of the universal presence of the penis. But now the paths of the sexes divide. The boy enters the Œdipus phase; he begins to manipu-

---

[7] The question arises whether satisfaction of purely destructive instinctual impulses can be felt as pleasure, whether pure destructiveness without any libidinal component occurs. Satisfaction of what remains in the ego of the death instinct seems not to produce feelings of pleasure, although masochism represents a fusion which is precisely analogous to sadism.

[8] The occurrence of early vaginal excitations is often asserted. But it is most probably a question of excitations in the clitoris, that is, in an organ analogous to the penis, so that this fact would not preclude us from describing the phase as phallic.

late his penis, and simultaneously has phantasies of carrying out some sort of activity with it in relation to his mother; but at last, owing to the combined effect of a threat of castration and the spectacle of women's lack of a penis, he experiences the greatest trauma of his life, and this introduces the period of latency with all its attendant consequences. The girl, after vainly attempting to do the same as the boy, comes to recognize her lack of a penis or rather the inferiority of her clitoris, with permanent effects upon the development of her character; and, as a result of this first disappointment in rivalry, she often turns away altogether from sexual life.

It would be a mistake to suppose that these three phases succeed one another in a clear-cut fashion: one of them may appear in addition to another, they may overlap one another, they may be present simultaneously.

In the earlier phases the separate component instincts set about their pursuit of pleasure independently of one another; in the phallic phase there are the first signs of an organization which subordinates the other trends to the primacy of the genitals and signifies the beginning of a co-ordination of the general pursuit of pleasure into the sexual function. The complete organization is not attained until puberty, in a fourth, or genital, phase. A state of affairs is then established in which (1) many earlier libidinal cathexes are retained, (2) others are included in the sexual function as preparatory or auxiliary acts, their satisfaction producing what is known as fore-pleasure, and (3) other tendencies are excluded from the organization, and are either entirely suppressed (repressed) or are employed in the ego in some other way, forming character-traits or undergoing sublimation with a displacement of their aims.

This process is not always carried out perfectly. Inhibitions in the course of its development manifest themselves as the various disturbances of sexual life. Fixations of the libido to conditions at earlier phases are then found, the trend of which, moving independently of the normal sexual aim, is described as *perversion*. One example of an inhibition in development of this kind is homosexuality, if it is manifest. Analysis shows that in every case a homosexual attachment to an object has at one time been present and in most cases has persisted in a latent condition. The situation is complicated by the fact that the processes necessary for bringing about a normal outcome are not for the most part either completely present or completely absent; they are as a rule *partially* present, so that the final result remains dependent upon *quantitative* relations. Thus genital organization will be attained, but will be weakened in respect of those portions of the libido which have not proceeded so far but have remained fixated to pregenital objects and aims. Such weakening shows itself in a tendency, if there is an absence of genital satisfaction or if there are difficulties in the real world, for the libido to return to its earlier pregenital cathexes (*i.e.* to *regress*).

During the study of the sexual functions it has been possible to gain a first, preliminary conviction, or rather suspicion, of two pieces of knowledge which will later be found to be important over the whole of our field. Firstly, the normal and abnormal phenomena that we observe (that is, the phenomenology of the subject) require to be described from the point of view of dynamics and of economics (*i.e.*, in this connection, from the point of view of the quantitative distribution of the libido). And secondly, the etiology of the disturbances which we are studying is to be found in the developmental history of the individual, that is to say, in the early part of his life.

CHAPTER FOUR

Mental Qualities

WE HAVE described the structure of the psychical apparatus and the energies or forces which are active in it, and we have followed in a striking example the way in which those energies (and principally the libido) organize themselves into a physiological function which serves the purpose of the preservation of the species. There was nothing in all this to exemplify the quite peculiar character of what is mental, apart, of course, from the empirical fact that this apparatus and these energies underlie the functions which we call our mental life. We will now turn to something which is a unique characteristic of what is mental, and which, in fact, according to a widely held opinion, actually coincides with it to the exclusion of all else.

The starting point for this investigation is provided by a fact without parallel, which defies all explanation or description—the fact of consciousness. Nevertheless, if anyone speaks of consciousness, we know immediately and from our own most personal experience what is meant by it.[9] Many people, both inside and outside the science of psychology, are satisfied with the assumption that consciousness alone is mental, and nothing then remains for psychology but to discriminate in the phenomenology of the mind between perceptions, feelings, intellective processes and volitions. It is generally agreed, however, that these conscious processes do not form unbroken series which are complete in themselves; so that there is no alternative to assuming that there are physical or somatic processes which accompany the mental ones and which must admittedly be more complete than the mental series, since some of them have conscious processes parallel to them but others have not. It thus seems natural to lay the stress in psychology upon these somatic processes, to see in *them* the true essence of what is mental and to try to arrive at some other assessment of the conscious processes. The majority of philosophers, however, as well as many other people, dispute this position and

---

[9] Extreme lines of thought, such as the American doctrine of behaviorism, think it possible to construct a psychology which disregards this fundamental fact.

❧ 34 ❧

declare that the notion of a mental thing being unconscious is self-contradictory.

But it is precisely this that psychoanalysis is obliged to assert, and this is its second fundamental hypothesis. It explains the supposed somatic accessory processes as being what is essentially mental and disregards for the moment the quality of consciousness. It does not stand alone in this opinion. Many thinkers (such as Theodor Lipps, for instance) have made the same assertion in the same words. And the general dissatisfaction with the usual view of what is mental has resulted in an ever more urgent demand for the inclusion in psychological thought of a concept of the unconscious, though the demand has been of such an indefinite and vague nature that it could have no influence upon science.

Now it might appear as though this dispute between psychoanalysis and philosophy was only concerned with a trifling matter of definition—the question whether the name "mental" should be applied to one or another series of phenomena. Actually, however, this step has been of the greatest importance. Whereas the psychology of consciousness never went beyond this broken sequence of events which was obviously dependent upon something else, the other view, which held that what is mental is in itself unconscious, enabled psychology to take its place as a natural science like any other. The processes with which it is concerned are in themselves just as unknowable as those dealt with by the other sciences, by chemistry or physics, for example; but it is possible to establish the laws which those processes obey and to follow over long and unbroken stretches their mutual relations and interdependences—in short, to gain what is known as an "understanding" of the sphere of natural phenomena in question. This cannot be effected without framing fresh hypotheses and creating fresh concepts; but these are not to be despised as evidence of our embarrassment but must on the contrary be valued as enriching science. We can claim for them the same value as approximations as belongs to the corresponding intellectual scaffolding found in other natural sciences, and we look forward to their being modified, corrected and more precisely determined as more experience is accumulated and sifted. So too it will be entirely in accordance with our expectations if the basic concepts and principles of the new science (instinct, nervous energy, etc.) remain for a considerable time no less indeterminate than those of the older sciences (force, mass, attraction, etc.).

Every science is based upon observations and experiences arrived at through the medium of our psychical apparatus. But since *our* science has as its subject that apparatus itself, the analogy ends here. We make our observations through the medium of the same perceptual apparatus, precisely by the help of the breaks in the series of [conscious] mental events, since we fill in the omissions by plausible inferences and translate them into conscious material. In this way we construct, as it were, a series of conscious events complementary to the unconscious mental processes. The relative certainty of our mental science rests upon the binding force of these inferences. Anyone who goes deeply into the subject will find that our technique holds its ground against every criticism.

In the course of our work the distinctions which we denote as *mental qualities* force themselves on our attention. There is no need to characterize what we call *conscious*: it is the same as the consciousness of philosophers and of everyday opinion. Everything else that is mental is in our view *unconscious*. We are soon led to make an important division in this unconscious. Some processes become conscious easily; they may then cease to be conscious, but can become conscious once more without any trouble: as people say, they can be reproduced or remembered. This reminds us that consciousness is in general a very highly fugitive condition. What is conscious is conscious only for a moment. If our perceptions do not confirm this, the contradiction is merely an apparent one. It is explained by the fact that the stimuli of perception can persist for some time, so that in the course of it the perception of them can be repeated. The whole position can be clearly seen from the conscious perception of our intellective processes; it is true that these may persist, but they may just as easily pass in a flash. Everything unconscious that behaves in this way, that can easily exchange the unconscious condition for the conscious one, is therefore better described as "capable of entering consciousness," or as *preconscious*. Experience has taught us that there are hardly any mental processes, even of the most complicated kind, which cannot on occasion remain preconscious, although as a rule they press forward, as we say, into consciousness. There are other mental processes or mental material which have no such easy access to consciousness, but which must be inferred, discovered, and translated into conscious form in the manner that has been described. It is for such material that we reserve the name of the unconscious proper.

Thus we have attributed three qualities to mental processes: they are either conscious, preconscious, or unconscious. The division between the three classes of material which have these qualities is neither absolute nor permanent. What is preconscious becomes conscious, as we have seen, without any activity on our part; what is unconscious can, as a result of our efforts, be made conscious, though in the process we may have an impression that we are overcoming what are often very strong resistances. When we make an attempt of this kind upon someone else, we ought not to forget that the conscious filling up of the breaks in his perceptions—the construction which we are offering him—does not so far mean that we have made conscious in him the unconscious material in question. All that is so far true is that the material is present in his mind in two versions, first in the conscious reconstruction that he has just received and secondly in its original unconscious condition. By persistent efforts we usually succeed in bringing it about that this unconscious material too becomes conscious to him, as a result of which the two versions come to coincide. The amount of effort needed, by which we estimate the resistance against the material becoming conscious, varies in magnitude in each individual case. For instance, what comes about in an analytic treatment as the result of our efforts can also occur spontaneously: material which is ordinarily unconscious can transform itself into preconscious and then into conscious material—a thing that happens upon a large scale in psychotic states. From this we may infer that the maintenance of certain internal resistances is a *sine qua non* of normality. A lowering of resistances of this sort, with a consequent pressing forward of unconscious material, takes place regularly in the state of sleep and thus brings about a necessary precondition for the formation of dreams.

On the other hand, preconscious material can become temporarily inaccessible and cut off by resistances, as on occasions of passing forgetfulness, or a preconscious thought can actually be temporarily pushed back into the unconscious condition, as seems to be necessary in the case of jokes. We shall see that a similar reversion of preconscious material or processes to the unconscious condition plays a great part in the causation of neurotic disorders.

The theory of the three qualities of mental events, as described in this generalized and simplified manner, seems likely to be a source of endless confusion rather than a help to clarification. But it must not be forgotten that it is properly not a theory at all, but a first attempt at a stock-taking of the facts of our observation, that it keeps as close as possible to those facts and does not seek to explain them. The complications which it reveals may bring into relief the peculiar difficulties with which our investigation has to contend. It seems likely however that we shall learn more about the subject if we follow out the relations between the mental qualities and the provinces or agencies which we have postulated in the mental apparatus—though these relations too are far from being simple.

The process of a thing becoming conscious is above all linked with the perceptions which our sense organs receive from the external world. From the topographical point of view, therefore, it is a phenomenon which occurs in the outermost cortex of the ego. It is true that we also receive conscious information from the inside of the body—the feelings, which actually exercise a more peremptory influence upon our mental life than external perceptions; moreover, in certain circumstances the sense organs themselves transmit feelings, sensations of pain, in addition to the perceptions which are specific to them. Since, however, these feelings (as we call them, in contrast to conscious perceptions) also emanate from the terminal organs, and since we regard all of those organs as prolongations or offshoots of the cortex, it is still possible to maintain the assertion made at the beginning of this paragraph. It need only be said by way of distinction that, as regards the terminal organs of *feeling*, the body itself takes the place of the external world.

Conscious processes on the periphery of the ego and everything else in the ego unconscious—such would be the simplest state of affairs that we might picture. And such may in fact be the conditions prevailing in animals. But in men there is an added complication owing to which internal processes in the ego may also acquire the quality of consciousness. This complication is produced by the function of speech, which brings the material in the ego into a firm connection with the memory-traces of visual and more particularly of auditory perceptions. Thenceforward the perceptual periphery of the cortex of the ego can be stimulated to a much greater extent from inside as well; internal events such as sequences of ideas and intellective processes can become conscious; and a special apparatus becomes necessary in order to distinguish between the two possibilities—that is, what is known as *reality-testing*. The equation "perception = reality (external world)" no longer holds. Errors, which can now easily arise and do in fact habitually arise in dreams, are called *hallucinations*.

The inside of the ego, which comprises above all the intellective processes, has the quality of being preconscious. This is characteristic of the ego and belongs to it alone. It would not be right, however, to assert that a connection with the memory-traces of speech is a prerequisite of the preconscious condition. On the contrary, that condition does not depend upon any such prerequisite, although the presence of speech gives a safe clue to the preconscious nature of a process. The preconscious condition, which is characterized on the one hand by having access to consciousness and on the other hand by being linked with the verbal residues, is nevertheless something peculiar, the nature of which is not exhausted by these two characteristics. The proof of this is that large portions of the ego, and in particular of the superego, which cannot be denied the characteristic of being preconscious, none the less remain for the most part unconscious in the phenomenological sense of the word. We do not know why this must be so. We shall attempt later on to attack the problem of the true nature of the preconscious.

The sole quality that rules in the id is that of being unconscious. Id and unconscious are as intimately united as ego and preconscious; indeed, the former connection is even more exclusive. If we look back at the developmental history of the individual and of his psychical apparatus, we shall be able to make an important distinction in the id. Originally, of course, everything was id; the ego was developed out of the id by the continual influence of the external world. In the course of this slow development certain material in the id was transformed into the preconscious condition and was thus taken into the ego. Other material remained unaltered in the id, as its hardly accessible nucleus. But during this development the young and feeble ego dropped and pushed back into the unconscious condition certain material which it had already taken in, and behaved similarly in regard to many new impressions which it *might* have taken in, so that these were rejected and were able to leave traces in the id only. In consideration of its origin, we term this portion of the id *the repressed*. It is of little importance that we are not always able to draw a sharp distinction between these two categories of material in the id. They coincide approximately with the division between what was originally present and what was acquired during the development of the ego.

Having now decided upon the topographical division of the mental apparatus into an ego and an id, with which the difference in quality between preconscious and unconscious runs parallel, and having agreed that this quality is only an *indication* of the distinction and does not constitute its essence, we are faced by a further question. What is the true nature of the condition which is disclosed in the case of the id by the quality of being unconscious and in the case of the ego by that of being preconscious, and in what does the distinction between them consist?

But of this we know nothing; and the profound obscurity of our ignorance is scarcely illuminated by a glimmer or two of light. For here we have approached the still shrouded secret of the nature of what is mental. We assume, as the other natural sciences have taught us to expect, that in mental life some kind of energy is at work; but we have no data which enable us to come nearer to a knowledge of it by an analogy with other forms of energy. We seem to recognize that nervous or psychical energy exists in two forms, one freely mobile and the other, by contrast, bound; we speak of cathexes and hypercathexes of the material of the mind and even venture to suppose that a hypercathexis brings about a sort of synthesis of different processes— a synthesis in the course of which free energy is transformed into bound energy. Further than this we have been unable to go. Nevertheless, we hold firmly to the view that the distinction between the unconscious and the preconscious condition also lies in dynamic relations of this same kind, which would explain how it is that, whether spontaneously or with our assistance, the one can be changed into the other.

But behind all of these uncertainties there lies one new fact, the discovery of which we owe to psycho-analytic research. We have learned that processes in the unconscious or in the id obey different laws from those in the preconscious ego. We name these laws in their totality the *primary process*, in contrast to the *secondary process* which regulates events in the preconscious or ego. Thus the study of mental qualities has after all proved not unfruitful in the end.

CHAPTER FIVE

Dream-Interpretation as
an Illustration

AN INVESTIGATION of normal, stable states, in which the frontiers of the ego are safeguarded against the id by resistances (or anti-cathexes) and have held firm, and in which the superego is not distinguished from the ego because they work together harmoniously —an investigation of this kind would teach us little. The only things that can help us are states of conflict and rebellion, in which the material in the unconscious id has a prospect of forcing its way into the ego and into consciousness and in which the ego arms itself afresh against the invasion. Only under such conditions can we make observations which will confirm or correct our views upon the two partners. But our nightly sleep is precisely a state of this sort, and consequently our activity during sleep, which we perceive as dreams, is the most favorable object of our study. In this way, too, we avoid the familiar charge of basing our constructions of the normal life of the mind upon pathological findings; for dreams are regular events in the life of normal men, however much their characteristics may differ from the productions of our waking existence.

Dreams, as everyone knows, can be confused, unintelligible or positively senseless, their contents may contradict all that we know of reality, and we behave in them like insane people, since, so long as we are dreaming, we attribute objective reality to the material of our dreams. We can find our way toward understanding (or "interpreting") dreams, if we assume that what we recollect as the dream after we have waked up is not the true dream-process but only a façade behind which that process lies concealed. Here we have our distinction between *manifest* dream-material and *latent* dream-thoughts. The process which produces the former out of the latter is described as *dream-work*. The study of dream-work affords us an excellent example of the way in which unconscious material from the id—originally unconscious and repressed unconscious alike—forces itself upon the ego, becomes preconscious and, owing to the efforts of the ego, undergoes the modifications which we call *dream-distortion*. There are no features of the dream which cannot be explained in this fashion.

It is best to begin by pointing out that the formation of dreams can be provoked in two different ways. Either, on the one hand, an instinctual impulse which is as a rule suppressed (that is, an unconscious wish) finds enough strength during sleep to make an impression upon the ego, or, on the other hand, a desire left over from waking life, a preconscious chain of thought with all the conflicting impulses belonging to it, obtains reinforcement during sleep from an unconscious element. In short, dreams may arise either from the id or from the ego. The mechanism of dream-formation is the same in both cases and so is the necessary dynamic precondition. The ego gives evidence of its origin from the id by occasionally ceasing its functions and permitting a reversion to an earlier state of things. It duly brings this about by breaking off its relations with the external world and withdrawing its cathexes from the sense organs. We shall be justified in saying that there arises at birth an instinct to return to the intra-uterine life that has been abandoned—an instinct to sleep. Sleep is a return of this kind to the womb. Since the waking ego controls the power of movement, that function is paralyzed in sleep, and accordingly a great part of the inhibitions imposed upon the unconscious id becomes superfluous. The withdrawal or diminution of these anti-cathexes thus allows the id what is now a harmless degree of liberty. The evidence of the share taken by the unconscious id in the formation of dreams is abundant and convincing. (*a*) Memory is far more comprehensive in dreams than in waking life. Dreams bring up recollections which the dreamer has forgotten, which are inaccessible to him when he is awake. (*b*) Dreams make an unlimited use of linguistic symbols, the meaning of which is for the most part unknown to the dreamer. Our experience, however, enables us to establish their sense. They probably originate from earlier phases in the development of speech. (*c*) Memory very often reproduces in dreams impressions from the dreamer's early childhood of which we can definitely assert not only that they had been forgotten but that they had become unconscious owing to repression. This is the explanation of the help—usually indispensable—afforded to us by dreams when, in the course of the analytic treatment of the neuroses, we attempt to reconstruct the early life of the dreamer. (*d*) Beyond this, dreams bring to light material which could not originate either from the dreamer's adult life or from his forgotten childhood. We are obliged to regard it as part of the *archaic heritage* which a child brings with him into the world, before any experience of his own, as a result of the experiences of his ancestors. We find elements corresponding to this phylogenetic material in the earliest human legends and in surviving customs. Thus dreams offer a source of human prehistory which is not to be despised.

But what makes dreams so invaluable for giving us knowledge is the circumstance that, when the unconscious material forces its way into the ego, it carries along with it its own methods of working. That is to say, the preconscious thoughts in which the unconscious material has found its expression are treated in the course of dream-work as though they were unconscious portions of the id; and, in the case of the other method of the formation of dreams, the preconscious thoughts which have reinforced themselves with an unconscious instinctual impulse are reduced to the unconscious condition. It is only in this way that we can discover the laws that govern unconscious processes and the respects in which they differ from the rules that are familiar to us in waking thought. Thus dream-work is in its essence a case of an unconscious working-over of preconscious thought processes. To take an analogy from history: invading conquerors govern a conquered country, not according to the judicial system which they find in force there, but according to their own. But it is undeniable that the product of dream-work is a compromise. The ego-organization is not *y*et entirely paralyzed, and its influence is to be seen in the distortion imposed upon the unconscious material and in what is often a vain attempt at giving to the total result a shape that shall be not too unacceptable to the ego (by means of a secondary working-over or *secondary elaboration*). In our analogy this would be represented as signs of the continued resistance of the conquered people.

The laws governing unconscious processes, which come to light in this manner, are remarkable enough and suffice to explain the greater part of what seems strange to us about dreams. Above all there is a striking tendency to *condensation*, an inclination to form fresh unities out of elements which in our waking thoughts we should certainly have kept separate. As a consequence of this, a single element of the manifest dream often stands for a whole number of latent dream-thoughts, as though it were a combined allusion to all of them; and in general the dimensions of a manifest dream are extraordinarily small in comparison with the wealth of material from which it has sprung. Another peculiarity of dream-work, which is not completely divorced from the one already mentioned, is the ease with which mental intensities (or cathexes) are *displaced* from one element to another, so that it often happens that an element which was of no consequence in the dream-thoughts appears to be the clearest and accordingly the most important feature of the manifest dream, and, *vice versa*, that essential elements of the dream-thoughts are represented in the manifest dream by only the faintest allusions. Moreover, as a rule the existence of the most insignificant points in common between two elements is enough to enable the dream-work to replace one by the other for any other purpose. It will easily be imagined how greatly the difficulty of interpreting a dream and of revealing the relations between the manifest dream and the latent dream-thoughts can be increased by these mechanisms of condensation and displacement. From the evidence of the existence of these two tendencies toward condensation and displacement our theory infers that in the unconscious id the energy is in a condition of free mobility, and that the id sets more store by the opportunity of discharging quantities of excitation than it does by any other consideration; [10] and our theory makes use of these two peculiarities in defining the character of the primary process which we have ascribed to the id.

The study of dream-work has taught us many other equally remarkable and important characteristics of the processes in the unconscious; but we can only mention

---

[10] An analogy is afforded by the non-commissioned officer who accepts a reprimand from his superior in silence but vents his anger upon the first innocent private whom he happens to meet.

a few of them here. The governing laws of logic have no sway in the unconscious; it might be called the Kingdom of the Illogical. Impulses with contrary aims exist side by side in the unconscious without any call being made for an adjustment between them. Either they have no effect whatever upon each other, or, if they do, no decision is made, but a compromise comes about which is senseless since it embraces mutually exclusive elements. Similarly, contraries are not kept apart from each other but are treated as though they were identical, so that in the manifest dream any element may also stand for its contrary. Certain philologists have found that the same holds good in the oldest languages, and that contraries such as "strong-weak," "light-dark," "high-deep" were originally expressed by the same roots, until two different modifications of the primitive word distinguished the two meanings. Remains of this original double meaning seem to have survived even in such a highly developed language as Latin in the use of words like *altus* ("high" and "deep") and *sacer* ("holy" and "accursed").

In view of the complication and multiplicity of the relations between the manifest dream and the latent material lying behind it, it may of course justly be asked how it is at all possible to deduce the one from the other and whether we rely upon lucky guesses, helped perhaps by a translation of the symbols that occur in the manifest dream. It can be said in reply that in the great majority of cases the problem can be satisfactorily solved, but only with the assistance of the associations provided by the dreamer himself to the elements of the manifest material. Any other procedure is arbitrary and can give no certain result. But the dreamer's associations bring to light intermediate links which we can then insert in the gap between the two and with the help of which we can recover the latent material of the dream and "interpret" it. It is not to be wondered at that this work of interpretation (acting in a direction opposite to that of the dream-work) fails occasionally to find a completely certain conclusion.

It remains for us to give a dynamic explanation of why it is in the first instance that the sleeping ego takes upon itself the task of dream-work. That explanation is fortunately easy to find. With the help of the unconscious, every dream in the process of formation makes a demand upon the ego for the satisfaction of an instinct (if it originates from the id) or for the solution of a conflict, the removal of a doubt, or the making of a decision (if it originates from a residue of preconscious activity in waking life). The sleeping ego, however, is focused upon the wish to maintain sleep; it regards this demand as a disturbance and seeks to get rid of the disturbance. The ego achieves this by what appears to be an act of compliance: it meets the demand with what is in the circumstances the innocent fulfillment of a wish and thus disposes of the demand. This replacement of a demand by the fulfillment of a wish remains the essential function of dream-work. It is perhaps worth while to illustrate this by three simple examples—a hunger dream, a dream of convenience, and a dream arising out of sexual desire. During his sleep a need for food stirs in the dreamer. He has a dream of a delicious meal and sleeps on. The choice, of course, was open to him of either waking up and eating something or of continuing his sleep. He decided in favor of the latter and satisfied his hunger by means of the dream: at all events for the time being— since if his hunger had persisted he would have had to wake up nevertheless. Here is the second example. The sleeper must wake up in order to be in time for his work at the hospital. But he sleeps on, and has a dream that he is at the hospital—but as a patient, who has no need to get up. Or again, a desire arises during the night for the enjoyment of a forbidden sexual object—a friend's wife. The sleeper dreams of sexual intercourse—not, however, with this particular person but with someone else of the same name to whom he is in fact quite indifferent; or his objection to the desire may find expression in his mistress remaining completely anonymous.

Naturally every case is not so simple. Especially in those dreams that arise from residues of the previous day which have not been dealt with and which have merely obtained reinforcement during sleep from the unconscious, it is often hard to detect the unconscious motive force and its wish-fulfillment; but we may assume that it is always there. The assertion that dreams are wish-fulfillments will easily arouse scepticism when it is remembered how many dreams have a positively painful content or even wake the sleeper with anxiety, quite apart from the numerous dreams without any definite feeling-tone. But the objection based upon anxiety dreams cannot be sustained against analysis. It must not be forgotten that dreams are invariably the product of a conflict, that they are a kind of compromise structure. Something that is a satisfaction for the unconscious id may for that very reason be a cause of anxiety for the ego.

As the dream-work proceeds, at one time the unconscious will press forward more successfully, while at another time the ego will defend itself with greater energy. Anxiety dreams are mostly those whose material has undergone least distortion. If the demand made by the unconscious is too great, so that the sleeping ego is not in a position to ward it off by the means at its disposal, it abandons the wish to sleep and returns to waking life. We shall be taking all our observations into account if we say that every dream is an *attempt* to put aside a disturbance of sleep by means of a wish-fulfillment. The dream is thus the guardian of sleep. This attempt can be more or less completely successful; it can also fail—in which case the sleeper wakes up, apparently aroused by the dream itself. So, too, there are occasions when that excellent fellow the night watchman, whose business it is to guard the little township's sleep, has no alternative but to sound the alarm and rouse the sleeping townspeople.

We shall conclude these remarks with a statement that will justify the long time we have spent over the problem of the interpretation of dreams. Experience has shown that the unconscious mechanisms which we discovered from our study of dream-work and which gave us an explanation of the formation of dreams also help us to understand the puzzling symptoms which attract our interest to neuroses and psychoses. A coincidence of such a kind cannot fail to excite high hopes in us.

PART TWO

The Practical Task

CHAPTER SIX

The Technique of Psychoanalysis

A DREAM, then, is a psychosis, with all the absurdities, delusions and illusions of a psychosis. No doubt it is a psychosis which has only a short duration, which is harmless and even performs a useful function, which is brought about with the subject's consent and is ended by an act of his will. Nevertheless it *is* a psychosis, and we learn from it that even so deep-going a modification of mental life as this can be undone and can give place to normal functioning. Is it too bold, then, to hope that it must also be possible to submit the dreaded spontaneous illnesses of the mind to our control and bring about their cure?

We already possess much knowledge preliminary to such an undertaking. We have postulated that it is the ego's task to meet the demands of the three forces upon which it is dependent—reality, the id and the super-ego—and meanwhile to preserve its own organization and maintain its own autonomy. The necessary condition for the pathological states we have mentioned can only be a relative or absolute weakening of the ego which prevents it from performing its tasks. The severest demand upon the ego is probably the keeping down of the instinctual claims of the id, and for this end the ego is obliged to maintain great expenditures of energy upon anti-cathexes. But the claims made by the superego, too, may become so powerful and so remorseless that the ego may be crippled, as it were, for its other tasks. We may suspect that, in the economic conflicts which now arise, the id and the superego often make common cause against the hard-pressed ego, which, in order to retain its normal state, clings on to reality. But if the other two are too strong, they may succeed in loosening the organization of the ego and altering it so that its proper relation to reality is disturbed or even abolished. We have seen it happen in dreams: when the ego is detached from the reality of the external world, then, under the influence of the internal world, it slips down into psychosis.

Our plan of cure is based upon these views. The ego

has been weakened by the internal conflict; we must come to its aid. The position is like a civil war which can only be decided by the help of an ally from without. The analytical physician and the weakened ego of the patient, basing themselves upon the real external world, are to combine against the enemies, the instinctual demands of the id, and the moral demands of the super-ego. We form a pact with each other. The patient's sick ego promises us the most complete candor, promises, that is, to put at our disposal all of the material which his self-perception provides; we, on the other hand, assure him of the strictest discretion and put at his service our experience in interpreting material that has been influenced by the unconscious. Our knowledge shall compensate for his ignorance and shall give his ego once more mastery over the lost provinces of his mental life. This pact constitutes the analytic situation.

No sooner have we taken this step than we meet with a first disappointment, a first warning against complacency. If the patient's ego is to be a useful ally in our common work, it must, however hard it may be pressed by the hostile powers, have retained a certain degree of coherence, a fragment at least of understanding for the demands of reality. But this is not to be expected from the ego of a psychotic; it cannot carry out a pact of this sort, indeed it can scarcely engage in it. It will very soon toss us away and the help we offer it, to join the portions of the external world that no longer mean anything to it. Thus we learn that we must renounce the idea of trying our plan of cure upon psychotics— renounce it forever, perhaps, or only for the moment, until we have discovered some other plan better suited for that purpose.

But there is another class of psychological patients who evidently resemble the psychotics very closely, the immense number of sufferers from severe neuroses. The causes as well as the pathogenic mechanisms of their illness must be the same or at least very similar. Their ego, however, has proved more resistant and has become less disorganized. Many of them, in spite of their troubles and of their consequent inadequacy, are none the less able to maintain their position in real life. It may be that these neurotics will show themselves ready to accept our help. We will confine our interest to them and see how far and by what means we can "cure" them.

We conclude our pact then with the neurotics: complete candor on one side, strict discretion on the other. This looks as though we were aiming at the post of a secular father confessor. But there is a great difference, for what we want to hear from our patient is not only what he knows and conceals from other people, but what he does *not* know. With this end in view we give him a more detailed definition of what we mean by candor. We impose upon him the *fundamental rule* of analysis, which is henceforward to govern his behavior to us. He must tell us not only what he can say intentionally and willingly, what will give him relief like a confession, but everything else besides that his self-observation presents him with—everything that comes into his head, even if it is *disagreeable* to say it, even if it seems *unimportant* or positively *meaningless*. If he can succeed after this injunction in putting his self-criticism out of action, he will provide us with a mass of material—thoughts, ideas, recollections—which already lie under the influence of the unconscious, which are often its direct derivatives, and which thus put us in a position to conjecture the nature of his repressed unconscious material and to extend, by the information we give him, his ego's knowledge of his unconscious.

But nothing could be further from the truth than that his ego is content to play the part of obediently and passively bringing us the material we require and of believing and accepting our translation of it. Very different things happen in fact, some of which we might have foreseen but others of which are bound to astonish us. The most remarkable is this. The patient is not satisfied with regarding the analyst in the light of reality as a helper and adviser who, moreover, is remunerated for the trouble he takes and who would himself be content with some such rôle as that of an Alpine guide on a difficult climb; on the contrary, the patient sees in his analyst the return—the reincarnation—of some important figure out of his childhood or past, and consequently transfers on to him feelings and reactions that undoubtedly applied to this model. It soon becomes evident that this fact of transference is a factor of undreamed-of importance—on the one hand an instrument of irreplaceable value and on the other a source of serious dangers. This transference is *ambivalent*: it comprises positive and affectionate as well as negative and hostile attitudes toward the analyst, who, as a rule, is put in the place of one or other of the patient's parents, his father or his mother. So long as it is positive it serves us admirably. It alters the whole analytic situation and sidetracks the patient's rational aim of becoming well and free from his troubles. Instead of it there emerges the aim of pleasing the analyst, of winning his applause and his love. This becomes the true motive-force for the patient's collaboration; the weak ego becomes strong; under the influence of this aim the patient achieves things that would otherwise be beyond his power; his symptoms disappear and he seems to have recovered—all of this simply out of love for his analyst. The analyst must shamefacedly admit to himself that he set out upon a difficult undertaking without any suspicion of the extraordinary powers that would be at his command.

Moreover, the relation of transference carries with it two further advantages. If the patient puts the analyst in the place of his father (or mother), he is also giving him the power which his superego exercises over his ego, since his parents were, as we know, the origin of his superego. The new superego now has an opportunity for a sort of *after-education* of the neurotic; it can correct blunders for which his parental education was to blame. But at this point a warning must be given against misusing this new influence. However much the analyst may be tempted to act as teacher, model and ideal to other people and to make men in his own image, he should not forget that that is not his task in the analytic relationship, and indeed that he will be disloyal to his task if he allows himself to be led on by his inclinations. He will only be repeating one of the mistakes of the parents, when they crushed their child's independence, and he will only be replacing one kind of dependence by another. In all his attempts at improving and educating the patient the analyst must respect his individuality. The amount of influence which he may legitimately employ will be determined by the degree of inhibition in development present in the patient. Many neurotics have remained so infantile that in analysis too they can only be treated as children.

Another advantage of transference is that in it the patient produces before us with plastic clarity an important part of his life history, of which he would otherwise have probably given us only an unsatisfactory account. It is as though he were acting it in front of us instead of reporting it to us.

And now for the other side of the question. Since transference reproduces the patient's relation with his parents, it takes over the ambivalence of that relation as well. It almost inevitably happens that one day his positive attitude toward the analyst changes over into a negative and hostile one. This too is as a rule a repetition of the past. His obedience to his father (if it is his father that is in question), his wooing his father's favor, have their roots in an erotic wish directed toward him. Sometime or other this demand will press its way up in the transference as well and insist upon satisfaction. But in the analytic situation it must necessarily meet with frustration. Real sexual relations between patients and analysts are impossible, and even subtler methods of satisfaction, such as favors, intimacy, and so on, will be only sparingly granted by the analyst. A humiliation of this kind is taken as the occasion for the change-over; the same thing probably occurred in the patient's childhood.

Therapeutic successes that take place under the sway of the positive transference are under the suspicion of being of a *suggestive* nature. If the negative transference gains the upper hand they are blown away like spray before the wind. We perceive with horror that all our trouble and labor hitherto have been vain. Indeed, even what we had taken for a permanent intellectual gain by the patient, his understanding of psychoanalysis and his reliance upon its efficacy, suddenly vanishes. He behaves like a child who has no power of judgment of his own but blindly believes whoever he loves and no one else. The danger of these states of transference evidently consists in the possibility of the patient misunderstanding their nature and taking them for fresh real experiences instead of reflections of the past. If he (or she) perceives the strong erotic desire that lies concealed behind the positive transference, he believes that he has fallen passionately in love; if the transference changes over, then he feels himself insulted and neglected, he hates the analyst as an enemy and is ready to abandon the analysis. In both of these extreme cases he has forgotten the pact into which he entered at the beginning of the treatment and has become disqualified for continuing the common work. It is the analyst's task to tear the patient away each time from the menacing illusion, to show him again and again that what he takes to be new real life is a reflection of the past. And, to prevent him from falling into a state in which he will be inaccessible to all evidence, the analyst takes care that neither the love nor the hostility reach extreme heights. This is achieved by forewarning the patient in good time of these possibilities and by not overlooking the first signs of their appearance. Careful handling of the transference is as a rule richly rewarded. If we succeed, as we usually can, in persuading the patient of the true nature of the phenomena of transference, we have struck a powerful weapon out of the hand of his resistance and have converted dangers into gains. For the patient never forgets again what he has experienced in the form of transference; it has a greater force of conviction for him than anything that he can acquire in other ways.

It is a most undesirable thing if the patient *acts* outside the transference instead of remembering. The ideal conduct for our purposes would be that he should behave as normally as possible outside the treatment and express his abnormal reactions only in the transference.

The method by which we strengthen the patient's weakened ego has as its starting point an increase in the ego's self-knowledge. No doubt this is not the whole story, but it is a first step. The loss of such knowledge means for the ego a surrender of power and influence; it is the first tangible sign that the ego is being constricted and hampered by the demands of the id and of the superego. Thus the first part of the help we have to offer is intellectual work on our side and encouragement of the patient to collaborate in it. We are aware that this first kind of activity must pave the way to another more difficult problem. We shall not lose sight of the dynamic side of that problem even during our preliminary work. We obtain our material from a variety of sources—from what is provided by the information given by the patient and by his free associations, from what he shows us in his transferences, from what we gather by interpreting his dreams and from what he betrays by slips or *parapraxes*. All of this material helps us to make constructions in regard to what happened to him but has been forgotten, as well as in regard to what is now happening in him without his understanding it. But we never fail in all this to make a severe distinction between *our* knowledge and *his* knowledge. We avoid telling him at once things that we have often discovered quite early, or we avoid telling him the whole of what we think we have discovered. We consider carefully the moment at which we shall impart the knowledge of our constructions to him; we wait for what seems to be a suitable occasion—a judgment which it is not always easy to make. As a rule we put off telling him of a construction or explanation until he himself has so nearly arrived at it that only a single step remains to be taken, though that step is in fact the decisive synthesis. If we proceeded in another way and overwhelmed him with our interpretations before he was prepared for them, our information would either produce no effect or it would arouse a violent outbreak of *resistance* which would make the further progress of our work more difficult or might even threaten to stop it altogether. But if we have prepared everything properly, it often happens that our patient will immediately confirm our construction and himself recollect the internal or external event which he had forgotten. The more exactly the construction coincides with the details of what has been forgotten the easier will be his assent. As regards this particular matter *our* knowledge will then have become *his* knowledge as well.

With the mention of resistance we have reached the second and more important part of our task. We have already heard that the ego protects itself against the incursion of undesirable elements from the unconscious and repressed id by means of anti-cathexes, which must remain intact if it is to function normally. The more hardly the ego feels itself pressed, the more convulsively it clings (in terror, as it were) to these anti-cathexes, in order to protect what remains of it from further irruptions. But such defensive trends do not by any means harmonize with the aims of our treatment. We desire, on the contrary, that the ego, emboldened by the certainty of our help, shall dare to take the offensive in order to reconquer what has been lost. And it is at this point that we become aware of the strength of these anti-cathexes in the form of *resistances* against our work. The ego shrinks from undertakings that seem dangerous and threaten unpleasure; it must be constantly spurred on and soothed down if it is not to fail us. This resistance, which persists through the whole treatment and is renewed with every fresh piece of work, has been named, though not quite correctly, *repression-resistance*. We shall hear that it is not the only kind of resistance that meets us. It is interesting to notice that in this situation the allegiance of the different parties is in a sense reversed: for the ego is struggling against our appeal, while the unconscious, which is in general our opponent, comes to our help, since it has a natural "upward drive" and desires nothing better than to press forward across its ordained frontiers into the ego and into consciousness. The struggle which develops, if we gain our point and can persuade the ego to overcome its resistances, is carried through under our direction and with our assistance. Its outcome is a matter of indifference: whether it results in the ego accepting, after having made a fresh examination, an instinctual demand which it has hitherto repudiated, or whether it once more rejects it, this time finally. In either case a permanent danger has been disposed of, the compass of the ego has been extended and a wasteful expenditure of energy has been made unnecessary.

The overcoming of resistances is the part of our work which requires the greatest time and the greatest trouble. But it is worth while, since it brings about a favorable modification of the ego which will be maintained whatever the fate of the transference and will persist through the patient's life. And we have at the same time worked in the direction of undoing the modification which had been brought about under the influence of the unconscious; for whenever we have been able to detect its derivatives in the ego, we have drawn attention to their illegitimate origin and have urged the ego to eject them. It will be remembered that one of the essential conditions of our pact of assistance was that modifications of the ego of this kind, due to the intrusion of unconscious elements, should not have gone beyond a certain degree.

The further our work proceeds and the deeper our knowledge of the mental life of neurotics penetrates, the more clearly two new factors force themselves upon our notice which demand the closest attention as sources of resistance. Both of them are completely unknown to the patient, neither of them could be taken into account when our pact was made; nor do they arise from the patient's ego. They can both be included under the one description of "need to be ill" or "need to suffer"; but they are of different origins, though in other respects of a similar nature. The first of these two factors is the sense of guilt or consciousness of guilt, as it is called in disregard of the fact that the patient does not feel it and is not aware of it. It is evidently the portion of the resistance contributed by a superego that has grown peculiarly severe and cruel. The patient must not be healthy, he must remain ill, for he deserves no better. This resistance does not actually interfere with our intellectual work, but it makes it ineffective; indeed, it often allows us to remove one form of neurotic suffering but is ready to replace it at once by another one, or perhaps by an organic illness. The sense of guilt also offers an explanation of the cure or improvement of severe neuroses which we sometimes observe after real accidents: all that matters is that the patient should be wretched— in what way is of no consequence. The uncomplaining resignation with which such people often put up with their hard fate is most remarkable but also most revealing. In dealing with this resistance we are obliged to restrict ourselves to making it conscious and attempting the gradual demolition of the hostile superego.

It is not so easy to demonstrate the existence of yet another form of resistance, our means of combating which are especially inadequate. There are some neurotics in whom, to judge by all their reactions, the instinct of self-preservation has actually been reversed. They seem to have nothing in view but self-injury and self-destruction. It is possible that people who in the end do in fact commit suicide belong to this group. It must be supposed that in such people far-reaching defusions of instinct have taken place, as a result of which there have been set free excessive quantities of the destructive instinct directed inwards. These patients cannot tolerate the possibility of being cured by our treatment and fight against it with all their force. But it must be confessed that these are cases which we have not yet succeeded in explaining completely.

Let us once more glance over the situation which we have reached in our attempt at bringing help to the patient's neurotic ego. That ego is no longer able to fulfill the task set to it by the external world (including human society). It has not access to all of its experiences, a large proportion of its fund of memories have escaped it. Its activity is inhibited by the strict prohibitions of the superego, its energy is consumed in vain attempts at fending off the demands of the id. Beyond this, as a result of the constant inroads of the id, its organization is impaired, it is internally split apart, it is no longer capable of any proper synthesis, it is torn by discordant impulses, unappeased conflicts and unsolved doubts. To begin with, we induce the patient's thus enfeebled ego to take part in the purely intellectual work of interpretation, which aims at provisionally filling the gaps in his mental resources, and to transfer to us the authority of his superego; we stimulate his ego to take up the struggle over each individual demand made by the id and to defeat the resistances which arise in connection with it. At the same time, we restore order in his ego, by detecting the material and impulses which have forced their way in from the unconscious, and expose them to criticism by tracing them back to their origin. We serve the patient in various functions as an authority and a substitute for his parents, as a teacher and educator; and we have done the best for him if, as analysts, we raise the mental processes in his ego to a normal level, transform what had become unconscious and repressed into preconscious material and thus return it once more to the possession of his ego. On the patient's side certain rational factors operate in our favor, such as the need for recovery which arises from his sufferings and the intellectual interest that we may awaken in him in the theories and revelations of psychoanalysis; but of far greater force is the positive transference with which he meets us. On the other side there are fighting against us the negative transference, the ego's repression-resistance (that is, the unpleasure felt by it at undertaking the severe work imposed upon it), the sense of guilt arising from its relation to the superego, and the need to be ill caused by deep-going modifications in its instinctual economy. Whether we regard a case as slight or severe depends upon the share taken by the last two of these factors. Apart from these, there are a few other factors that may be mentioned as having a favorable or unfavorable influence. A particular kind of psychological inertia, a sluggishness of the libido, which is unwilling to abandon its fixations, is by no means welcome to us; the patient's capacity for sublimating his instincts plays an important part and the same is true of his capacity for rising superior to the crude life of the instincts as well as the relative power of his intellectual functions.

We shall not be disappointed, but on the contrary we shall find it entirely intelligible, if we are led to the conclusion that the final outcome of the struggle which we have engaged in depends upon *quantitative* relations, upon the amount of energy which we can mobilize in the patient to our advantage, in comparison with the amount of energy of the forces working against us. Here once more God is on the side of the big battalions. It is true that we do not always succeed in winning, but at least we can usually see why it is that we have not won. Those who have been following our discussion only out of therapeutic interest will perhaps turn away in contempt after this admission. But we are here concerned with therapy only in so far as it works by psychological methods; and for the time being we have no other. The future may teach us how to exercise a direct influence, by means of particular chemical substances, upon the amounts of energy and their distribution in the apparatus of the mind. It may be that there are other undreamed-of possibilities of therapy. But for the moment we have nothing better at our disposal than the technique of psychoanalysis, and for that reason, in spite of its limitations, it is not to be despised.

CHAPTER SEVEN

An Example of Psychoanalytical Work

❧ ❦❧
❧ ❦❧

WE HAVE formed a general picture of the psychical apparatus, of the portions, organs and agencies of which it is composed, of the forces which operate in it, and of the functions which its different portions perform. The neuroses and psychoses are states in which disturbances in the functioning of the apparatus come to expression. We have chosen the neuroses as the subject of our study because they alone seem to be accessible to the psychological methods of our approach. While we are endeavoring to influence them, we collect observations which give us a picture of their origin and of the manner in which they arise.

Let us state in advance one of our principal findings. Neuroses (unlike infectious diseases, for instance) have no specific determinants. It would be idle to seek in them for a pathogenic factor. They shade off into what is described as the normal by a series of transitional steps; and on the other hand there is scarcely any condition generally recognized as normal in which it would not be possible to demonstrate neurotic traits. Neurotics have approximately the same innate dispositions as other people, they have the same experiences and they have the same problems to solve. Why, then, do they live so much worse and with so much greater difficulty and suffer in the process so many more feelings of unpleasure, anxiety, and pain?

We have no need to feel at a loss for an answer to this question. It is *quantitative disharmonies* that must be held responsible for the inadequacies and sufferings of neurotics. The determining causes of all the varying forms of human mental life are to be looked for in the interplay between inherited dispositions and accidental experiences. Thus it may happen that one particular instinct is innately too strong or too weak, or that one particular capacity is stunted or insufficiently developed in life; while on the other hand it may happen that external impressions and experiences may make stronger demands upon one individual than upon another. What the constitution of one person can deal with may prove an unmanageable task for another. These quantitative differences are what will determine the variety of the results.

It will very soon be felt, however, that this explanation is unsatisfactory. It is too general, it explains too much. The etiology that has been put forward applies to every case of mental suffering, misery and disablement, but not every such state can be called neurotic. The neuroses have specific characteristics, they are misery of a particular sort. So we must after all expect to find specific causes for them. Or we might suppose that, among the tasks with which mental life has to deal, there are some in which it can especially easily fail; so that the peculiarity of the phenomena of neurosis, which are often so very remarkable, might follow from that fact, without any necessity for withdrawing our earlier assertions. If it remains true that the neuroses do not differ in any essential respect from the normal, their study promises to afford us useful contributions to our knowledge of the normal. It may be that we shall thus discover the "weak points" in a normal organization.

The supposition we have just made finds confirmation. Analytic experiences teach us that there actually is one instinctual demand the effort at dealing with which most easily fails or meets with only partial success, and that there is one period of life which comes into consideration exclusively or predominantly in connection with the origin of neuroses. These two factors—the nature of the instinct and the period of life in question—require to be treated separately, although they are often enough interconnected.

We can speak with a fair degree of certainty about the part played by the period of life. It seems that neuroses are only acquired during early childhood (up to the age of six), even though their symptoms may not make their appearance until much later. The infantile neurosis may become manifest for a short time or may be overlooked. In every case the subsequent neurotic illness has this prelude in childhood as its point of departure. (It is possible that what are known as traumatic neuroses—brought about by excessive fright or severe somatic shocks such as railway collisions, explosions, etc.—are an exception; their relation to the infantile factor has hitherto eluded investigation.) We can easily account for this preference for the first period of childhood. Neuroses are, as we know, disorders of the ego; and it is not to be wondered at that the ego, while it is weak, immature and incapable of resistance, should fail in dealing with problems which it could later manage with the utmost ease. (Instinctual demands from within operate as "traumas" no less than excitations from the external world, especially if they are met halfway by certain dispositions.) The helpless ego fends off these problems by attempts at flight (by *repressions*), which turn out later to be ineffective and which involve permanent hindrances to further development. The damage inflicted upon the ego by its first experiences may seem disproportionately great; but we have only to take as an analogy the differences in the effects produced by the prick of a needle upon a mass of germ cells during segmentation (as in Roux's experiments) and upon the complete animal which eventually develops out of them. No human individual is spared such traumatic experiences; none escapes the repressions to which they give rise. These hazardous reactions on the part of the ego may perhaps be indispensable for the attainment of another aim, which is bound up with the same period of life. In a few short years the little primitive creature must grow into a civilized human being; he must pass through an immensely long stretch of human cultural development in an almost uncannily abbreviated form. This is made possible by hereditary disposition; but it can scarcely ever be achieved without the additional help of education, of parental influence, which, as a precursor of the superego, restricts the activity of the ego by means of prohibitions and punishments and facilitates or compels the setting-up of repressions. We must not forget, therefore, to include the influence of civilization among the determinants of neuroses. It is easy, as we can see, for a barbarian to be healthy: for a civilized man the task is a hard one. The desire for a powerful and uninhibited ego may seem to us intelligible, but, as is shown by the times we live in, it is in the profoundest sense antagonistic to civilization. And since the demands of civilization are represented by family education, we must remember to find a place too in the etiology of the neuroses for this biological character of the human species—the prolonged period of its childhood dependence.

As regards the other point—the specific instinctual factor—we come upon an interesting discrepancy between theory and experience. Theoretically there is no objection to supposing that any sort of instinctual demand whatever could occasion these same repressions and their consequences; but our observation shows us invariably, so far as we can judge, that the excitations that play this pathogenic part arise from the component instincts of sexual life. The symptoms of neuroses are exclusively, it might be said, either a substitutive satisfaction of some sexual impulse or measures to prevent such a satisfaction, and are as a rule compromises between the two, of the kind that arise according to the laws operating between contraries in the unconscious. The gap in our theory cannot at present be filled; and our decision is made more difficult by the fact that most of the impulses of sexual life are not of a purely erotic nature but arise from alloys of the erotic instinct with components of the destructive instinct. But it cannot be doubted that the instincts which manifest themselves physiologically as sexuality play a prominent and unexpectedly large part in the causation of neuroses—whether an exclusive one, remains to be decided. It must also be borne in mind that in the course of cultural development no other function has been so energetically and extensively repudiated as precisely the sexual one. Theory must rest satisfied with a few hints that betray a deeper connection—the fact that the first period of childhood, during which the ego begins to be differentiated from the id, is also the period of early sexual efflorescence which is brought to an end by the period of latency, that it can hardly be a matter of chance that this momentous early period subsequently falls a victim to infantile amnesia, and finally that biological modifications in sexual life (such as its diphasic onset to which we have just referred, the disappearance of the periodic character of sexual excitement and the transformation in the relation between female menstruation and male excitation)—that these innovations in sexuality must have been of high importance in the evolution of animals into men. It is left for the science of the future to bring together these isolated data into a new understanding. It is not psychology but biology that is responsible for this gap. We shall not be wrong, perhaps, if we say that the weak point in the organization of the ego lies in its behavior toward the sexual function, as though the biological opposition between self-preservation and the preservation of the species there found psychological expression.

Since analytic experience has convinced us of the complete truth of the common assertion that the child is psychologically father of the man and that the events of his first years are of paramount importance for his whole subsequent life, we should be especially interested if there were something that could be described as the central experience of this period of childhood. Our attention is first attracted by the effects of certain influences which do not apply to all children, though they are common enough—such as the sexual abuse of children by adults, their seduction by other children (brothers or sisters) slightly their seniors, and, what is unexpected, the impression produced by seeing or overhearing sexual behavior between adults (their parents) mostly at a time at which one would not have thought they could either be interested in or understand any such impressions or be capable of remembering them later. It is easy to observe the extent to which a child's susceptibility is aroused by such experiences and how his own sexual impulses are thus forced into certain channels which they can never again leave. Since these impressions undergo repression, either immediately or as soon as they seek to return in the form of memories, they constitute a precondition for a neurotic compulsion which will subsequently make it impossible for the ego to control the sexual function and will probably cause it to turn away from that function permanently. The latter reaction will result in a neurosis; if it is absent, various perversions will emerge, or the function—vastly important as it is, not only for reproduction but for the entire shaping of life—will become wholly unmanageable.

However instructive such cases may be, our interest will be still more attracted by the influence of a situation which every child is fated to pass through and which follows inevitably from the factor of the length of his dependence in childhood and of his life with his parents. I am thinking of the *Œdipus complex*, so named because its essential substance is found in the Greek myth of King Œdipus, which has luckily been preserved for us in a version from the hand of a great dramatist. The Greek hero killed his father and married his mother. That he did so unknowingly, since he did not recognize them as his parents, constitutes a deviation from the analytical subject matter which is easily intelligible and indeed inevitable.

At this point we must give a separate account of the development of boys and girls (of men and women), since it is now that the difference between the sexes finds psychological expression for the first time. We are faced here by the great enigma of the biological fact of the duality of the sexes: for our knowledge it is something ultimate, it resists every attempt to trace it back to something else. Psychoanalysis has made no contribution toward solving this problem, which clearly falls entirely within the province of biology. In mental life we find only reflections of this great antithesis; and their interpretation is made more difficult by the fact, long suspected, that no individual is limited to the methods of reaction of a single sex but always finds some room for those of the opposite one, just as his body frequently bears, alongside the developed organs of one sex, the stunted and often useless rudiments of the other. For the purpose of distinguishing between male and female in mental life we assert an equivalence which is clearly insufficient, empirical, and conventional: we call everything that is powerful and active "male" and everything that is weak and passive "female." The fact of psychological bisexuality embarrasses all that we have to say on the subject and makes it more difficult to describe.

A child's first erotic object is the mother's breast that feeds him, and love in its beginnings attaches itself to the satisfaction of the need for food. To start with, the child certainly makes no distinction between the breast and his own body; when the breast has to be separated from his body and shifted to the "outside" because he so often finds it absent, it carries with it, now that it is an "*object*," part of the original narcissistic cathexis. This first object subsequently becomes completed into the whole person of the child's mother, who not only feeds him but also looks after him and thus arouses in him many other physical sensations pleasant and unpleasant. By her care of the child's body she becomes his first seducer. In these two relations lies the root of a mother's importance, unique, without parallel, laid down unalterably for a whole lifetime, as the first and strongest love-object and as the prototype of all later love relations—for both sexes. The phylogenetic foundation has so much the upper hand in all this over accidental personal experience that it makes no difference whether a child has really sucked at the breast or has been brought up on the bottle and never enjoyed the tenderness of a mother's care. His development takes the same path in both cases; it may be that in the latter event his later longing is all the greater. And for however long a child is fed at his mother's breast, he will always be left with a conviction after he is weaned that his feeding was too short and too little.

This preface is not without its uses, for it will prepare our minds for the intensity of the Œdipus complex. When a boy, from about the age of two or three, enters upon the phallic phase of his libidinal development, feels pleasurable sensations in his sexual organ and learns to procure these at will by manual stimulation, he becomes his mother's lover. He desires to possess her physically in the ways which he has divined from his observations and intuitive surmises of sexual life and tries to seduce her by showing her the male organ of which he is the proud owner. In a word, his early awakened masculinity makes him seek to assume, in relation to her, the place belonging to his father, who has hitherto been an envied model on account of the physical strength which he displays and of the authority in which he is clothed. His father now becomes a rival who stands in his way and whom he would like to push aside. If when his father is absent he is able to share his mother's bed and if when his father returns he is once more banished from it, his gratification when his father vanishes and his disappointment when he reappears are deeply felt experiences. This is the subject of the Œdipus complex, which Greek legend translated from the world of childhood phantasy into a pretended reality. Under the conditions of our civilization it is invariably doomed to a terrible end.

The boy's mother understands quite well that his sexual excitement refers to her. Sooner or later she thinks to herself that it is wrong to allow this state of things to continue. She believes she is acting rightly in forbidding him to manipulate his genitals. The prohibition has little effect and at the most brings about some modification in his method of self-gratification. At last his mother adopts the severest measures: she threatens to take away from him the thing he is defying her with. As a rule, in order to make the threat more terrifying and more credible, she delegates its carrying out to the boy's father, saying that she will tell him and that he will cut the penis off. Strangely enough, this threat only operates if another condition is fulfilled, either before or afterwards. In itself it seems quite inconceivable to the boy that anything of the sort could happen. But if when he is threatened he is able to recall the appearance of female genitals, or if shortly afterwards he has a glimpse of them—of genitals, that is to say, which really lack this supremely valued part, then he takes what he has heard seriously and, coming under the influence of the castration complex, experiences the severest trauma of his youthful existence.[11]

---

[11] Castration has a place, too, in the Œdipus legend, for the blinding with which Œdipus punished himself after the discovery of his crime is, by the evidence of dreams, a symbolic substitute for castration. The possibility cannot be excluded that a phylogenetic memory-trace may contribute to the extraordinarily terrifying effect of the threat—a memory-trace from the prehistory of the human family, when the jealous father would actually rob his son of his genitals if the latter interfered with him in rivalry for a woman. The primæval custom of circumcision, another symbolic substitute for castration,

The effects of the threat of castration are many and incalculable; they affect the whole of a boy's relations with his father and mother and subsequently with men and women in general. As a rule the child's masculinity is unable to stand up against this first shock. In order to preserve his sexual organs he gives up possession of his mother more or less completely; his sexual life often remains permanently under the weight of the prohibition. If a strong feminine component, as we put it, is present in him, its strength is increased by the threat to his masculinity. He falls into a passive attitude to his father, of a kind such as he ascribes to his mother. It is true that as a result of the threat he has given up masturbation, but not the activities of his imagination accompanying it. On the contrary, since they are now the only form of sexual gratification remaining to him, he practises them more than ever, and in these phantasies, while he continues as before to identify himself with his father, he also does so, simultaneously and perhaps predominantly, with his mother. Derivatives and modified products of these early masturbatory phantasies usually make their way into his later ego, and play a part in the formation of his character. Apart

---

is only intelligible if it is an expression of subjection to the father's will. (Compare the puberty rites of primitive peoples.) No investigation has yet been made of the form taken by the events described above among races and in civilizations which do not suppress masturbation among children.

from this encouragement of his femininity, fear and hatred of his father gain greatly in intensity. The boy's masculinity withdraws, as it were, into a defiant attitude toward his father, which in a compulsive fashion dominates his later behavior in human society. A residue of his erotic fixation to his mother is often left in the form of an excessive dependence upon her, and this persists as an attitude of subjection to women. He no longer ventures to love his mother, but he cannot risk not being loved by her, since in that case he would be in danger of being betrayed by her to his father and handed over to castration. The whole experience with all its antecedents and consequences, of which our account has only been able to give a selection, undergoes a highly energetic repression, and, as is made possible by the laws governing the unconscious id, all of the contending emotional impulses and reactions then set going are preserved in the unconscious, ready to disturb the later development of the ego after puberty. When the somatic process of sexual maturation puts new life into the old libidinal fixations which had apparently been surmounted, sexual life will be disclosed as inhibited, incoherent and fallen apart into mutually conflicting impulses.

It is no doubt true that the impact of the threat of castration upon a boy's budding sexual life does not always have these dreadful consequences. Once again it will depend upon *quantitative* relations how much damage is done and how much avoided. The whole occurrence, which may no doubt be regarded as the central experience of the years of childhood, the greatest problem of early life and the most important source of later inadequacy, is so completely forgotten that its reconstruction during the work of analysis is met by the adult's most determined scepticism. Indeed the objection to it is so great that it is sought to silence any mention of the tabooed subject, and the most obvious reminders of it are met with the strangest intellectual blindness. For instance, one hears the objection made that the legend of King Œdipus has in fact no connection with the construction made by analysis: the case was quite a different one, since Œdipus did not know that it was his father whom he killed and his mother whom he married. What is overlooked in this is that a distortion of this kind is unavoidable if an attempt is made at a poetic handling of the material, and that there is no addition of extraneous subject matter but merely a skillful employment of the factors present in the theme. The ignorance of Œdipus is a legitimate representation of the unconsciousness into which, for adults, the whole experience has fallen; and the doom of the oracle, which makes or should make the hero innocent, is a recognition of the inevitability of the fate which has condemned every son to live through the Œdipus complex. Again, it was pointed out by adherents of psychoanalysis that the enigma of another dramatic hero, Shakespeare's procrastinator, Hamlet, can be solved by a reference to the Œdipus complex, since he came to grief over the task of punishing someone else for what coincided with the substance of his own Œdipus wishes—whereupon the general lack of comprehension displayed by the literary world showed how ready is the mass of mankind to hold fast to its infantile repressions.[12]

Yet more than a century before the birth of psychoanalysis the French philosopher Diderot gave evidence of the importance of the Œdipus complex by expressing the difference between the primitive and civilized worlds in the following sentence: "Si le petit sauvage était abandonné à lui-même, qu'il conservât toute son imbécillité et qu'il réunît au peu de raison de l'enfant au berceau la violence des passions de l'homme de trente ans, il tordrait le cou à son père et coucherait

---

[12] The name "William Shakespeare" is most probably a pseudonym behind which there lies concealed a great unknown. Edward de Vere, Earl of Oxford, a man who has been regarded as the author of Shakespeare's works, lost a beloved and admired father while he was still a boy, and completely repudiated his mother, who contracted a new marriage soon after her husband's death.

avec sa mère." [13] I venture to assert that if psycho-analysis could boast of no other achievement than the discovery of the repressed Œdipus complex, that alone would give it a claim to be counted among the precious new acquisitions of mankind.

The effects of the castration complex upon little girls are more uniform and not less profound. A female child has, of course, no need to fear the loss of a penis; she must, however, react to the fact of not having received one. From the very first she envies boys its possession; her whole development may be said to take place under the influence of her envy for the penis. She begins by making vain attempts to do the same as boys and later, with greater success, makes efforts to compensate herself for the defect—efforts which may lead in the end to a normal feminine attitude. If during the phallic phase she attempts to get pleasure like a boy by the manual stimulation of her genitals, it often happens that she fails to obtain sufficient gratification and extends her judgment of inferiority from her stunted penis to her whole self. As a rule she soon gives up masturbating, since she does not wish to be reminded

---

[13] [From *Le Neveu de Rameau:* "If the little savage were left to himself, keeping all his foolishness and adding to the small sense of a babe in the cradle the violent passions of a man of thirty, he would strangle his father and lie with his mother."]

of the superiority of her brother or playmate, and turns away from sexuality altogether.

If a little girl adheres to her first wish—to grow into a boy—in extreme cases she will end as a manifest homosexual, and in any event will show markedly masculine traits in the conduct of her later life, will choose a masculine vocation, and so on. The other road leads by way of an abandonment of the mother she has loved: the daughter, under the influence of her envy for the penis, cannot forgive her mother for having sent her into the world so insufficiently equipped. In her resentment she gives her mother up and puts someone else in place of her as the object of her love—her father. If one has lost a love-object, the most obvious reaction is to identify oneself with it, to replace it, as it were, from within by means of identification. This mechanism now comes to the little girl's assistance. Identification with her mother can take the place of attachment to her mother. The little girl puts herself in her mother's place, as she has always done in her games; she tries to take her place with her father and begins to hate the mother whom she has hitherto loved, and from two motives: from jealousy as well as from mortification over the penis she has been denied. Her new relation to her father may begin by having as its content a wish to have his penis at her command; but it culminates in another wish—to have a baby from him as a present. The wish for a baby takes the place of the wish for a penis or at all events branches off from it.

It is an interesting thing that the relation between the Œdipus complex and the castration complex should be so different—should, indeed, be just the opposite—in the case of females and of males. In males, as we have seen, the threat of castration brings the Œdipus complex to an end; in females, on the contrary, we find that it is the effect of their lack of a penis that drives them into their Œdipus complex. It does little harm to a woman if she remains in her feminine Œdipus attitude. (The name of "Electra complex" has been proposed for it.) She will in that case choose her husband for his paternal characteristics and will be ready to recognize his authority. Her longing to possess a penis, which is in fact unappeasable, may be satisfied if she can succeed in completing her love for the organ by extending it to the man who bears that organ, just as earlier she progressed from her mother's breast to her mother as a whole.

If we ask an analyst what his experience has shown to be the mental structures least accessible to influence in his patients, the answer will be: in a woman, her desire for a penis, and in a man, his feminine attitude toward his own sex, a precondition of which would necessarily be the loss of his penis.

PART THREE

The Theoretical Yield

CHAPTER EIGHT

The Psychical Apparatus and the External World

ALL OF THE general views and assumptions which were brought forward in our first chapter were, of course, arrived at by laborious and patient detailed work of the sort of which we have given an example in the previous section. We may now feel tempted to make a survey of the increases in knowledge that we have achieved by work of this kind and to consider what paths lie open to us for further advances. In this connection we may be struck by the fact that we have so often been obliged to venture beyond the frontiers of the science of psychology. The phenomena with which we have had to deal do not belong only to psychology; they have also an organic and biological aspect, and accordingly in the course of our efforts at building up psychoanalysis we have also made important biological discoveries and have not been able to avoid framing new biological hypotheses.

But let us for the moment keep to psychology. We have found that it is not scientifically feasible to draw a line of demarcation between what is psychologically normal and abnormal; so that that distinction, in spite of its practical importance, possesses only a conventional value. We have thus established our right to arrive at an understanding of the normal life of the mind by studying its disorders—which would not be admissible if these pathological states, neuroses and psychoses, had specific causes, operating like foreign bodies.

The study of a mental disorder occurring during sleep, which is transient and harmless and which indeed performs a useful function, has given us the key to an understanding of the diseases of the mind which are permanent and injurious to life. And we may now venture to assert that the psychology of consciousness was no better able to understand the normal functioning of the mind than to understand dreams. The data of conscious self-perception, which were alone at its disposal, have proved themselves in every respect inadequate to fathom the profusion and complexity of the processes of the mind, to reveal their interconnections and so to arrive at the determining causes of disturbances of those processes.

We have adopted the hypothesis of a psychical apparatus, extended in space, appropriately constructed, developed by the exigencies of life, which gives rise to the phenomena of consciousness only at one particular point and under certain conditions. This hypothesis has put us in a position to establish psychology upon foundations similar to those of any other science, such as physics. In our science the problem is the same as in the others: behind the attributes (*i.e.* qualities) of the object under investigation which are directly given to our perception, we have to discover something which is more independent of the particular receptive capacities of our sense organs and which approximates more closely to what may be supposed to be the real state of things. There is no hope of our being able to reach the latter itself, since it is clear that everything new that we deduce must nevertheless be translated back into the language of our perceptions, from which it is simply impossible for us to set ourselves free. But in this lies the nature and limitation of our science. It is as though, in physics, we said: "If we could see clearly enough, we should find that what appear to be solid objects are made up of particles of such and such shape and size, occupying such and such relative positions."

So we endeavor to increase the efficiency of our sense organs as far as possible by artificial aids; but it is to be expected that such efforts will fail to affect the ultimate result. Reality will always remain "unknowable." What scientific work elicits from our primary sense perceptions will consist in an insight into connections and interdependences which are present in the external world, which can somehow or other be reliably reproduced or reflected in the internal world of our thoughts, and the knowledge of which enables us to "understand" something in the external world, to foresee it and possibly to alter it. Our procedure in psychoanalysis is exactly similar. We have discovered technical methods of filling up the gaps in the phenomena of our consciousness, and we make use of those methods just as a physicist makes use of experiment. In this manner we deduce a number of processes which are in themselves "unknowable" and insert them among the processes of which we are conscious. And if, for instance, we say: "At this point an unconscious memory intervened," what this means is: "At this point something occurred of which we are totally unable to form a conception, but which, if it had entered our consciousness, could only have been described in such and such a way."

Our justification for making such inferences and interpolations and the degree of certainty attaching to them of course remain open to criticism in each individual instance; and it is not to be denied that it is often exceedingly difficult to arrive at a decision—a fact which finds expression in the lack of agreement among analysts. The novelty of the problem is partly to blame for this, that is to say, lack of training. But there is besides this a special factor inherent in the subject itself; for in psychology, unlike physics, we are not always concerned with things which can only arouse a cold scientific interest. Thus we shall not be so very greatly surprised if a woman analyst who has not been sufficiently convinced of the intensity of her own desire for a penis also fails to assign an adequate importance to that factor in her patients. But such sources of error, arising from the personal equation, have, when all is said and done, no great significance. If one looks through old textbooks upon the use of the microscope, one is astonished to find the extraordinary demands which were placed upon the personality of those who made observations with that instrument while its technique was young, and of which there is no question today.

We cannot undertake in this place to attempt a complete picture of the psychical apparatus and of its functions; amongst other things we should find ourselves hindered by the circumstance that psychoanalysis has not yet had time to study all of those functions with equal attention. We shall therefore be content to give a detailed recapitulation of our account in the opening section.

The core of our being, then, is formed by the obscure *id*, which has no direct relations with the external world and is accessible even to our own knowledge only through the medium of another agency of the mind. Within this id the organic *instincts* operate, which are themselves composed of fusions of two primal forces (Eros and destructiveness) in varying proportions and are differentiated from one another by their relation to organs or systems of organs. The one and only endeavor of these instincts is toward satisfaction, which it is hoped to obtain from certain modifications in the organs by the help of objects in the external world. But an immediate and regardless satisfaction of instinct, such as the id demands, would often enough lead to perilous conflicts with the external world and to extinction. The id knows no precautions to ensure survival and no anxiety; or it would perhaps be more correct to say that, though it can produce the sensory elements of anxiety, it cannot make use of them. The processes which are possible in and between the assumed mental elements in the id (the *primary process*) differ largely from those which are familiar to us by conscious perception in our intellectual and emotional life; nor are they subject to the critical restrictions of logic, which repudiates some of these processes as invalid and seeks to undo them.

The id, which is cut off from the external world, has its own world of perception. It detects with extraordinary clarity certain changes in its interior, especially oscillations in the tension of its instinctual needs, oscillations which become conscious as feelings in the pleasure-unpleasure series. It is, to be sure, hard to say by what means and with the help of what sensory terminal organs these perceptions come about. But it remains certain that self-perceptions—cœnesthetic feelings and feelings of pleasure-unpleasure—govern events in the id with despotic force. The id obeys the inexorable pleasure principle. But not the id alone. It seems as though the activity of the other agencies of the mind is able only to modify the pleasure principle but not to nullify it; and it remains a question of the greatest theoretical importance, and one that has not yet been answered, when and how it is ever possible for the pleasure principle to be overcome. The consideration that the pleasure principle requires a reduction, or perhaps ultimately the extinction, of the tension of the instinctual needs (that is, a state of *Nirvana*) leads to problems that are still unexamined in the relations between the pleasure principle and the two primal forces, Eros and the death instinct.

The other agency of the mind, which we appear to

know the best and in which we recognize ourselves the most easily—what is known as the *ego*—was developed out of the cortical layer of the id, which, being adapted for the reception and exclusion of stimuli, is in direct contact with the external world. Starting from conscious perception, it has brought under its influence ever larger regions and ever deeper layers of the id; and, in the persistence with which it maintains its dependence upon the external world, it bears the indelible stamp of its origin (as it might be "Made in Germany"). Its psychological function consists in raising the processes in the id to a higher dynamic level (perhaps by transforming freely mobile into bound energy, such as corresponds to the preconscious condition); its constructive function consists in interposing, between the demand made by an instinct and the action that satisfies it, an intellective activity which, after considering the present state of things and weighing up earlier experiences, endeavors by means of experimental actions to calculate the consequences of the proposed line of conduct. In this way the ego comes to a decision whether the attempt to obtain satisfaction is to be carried out or postponed or whether it may not be necessary for the demand of the instinct to be altogether suppressed as being dangerous. (Here we have the *reality principle*.) Just as the id is directed exclusively to obtaining pleasure, so the ego is governed by considerations of safety. The ego has set itself the task of self-preservation, which the id appears to neglect. It makes use of sensations of anxiety as a signal to give a warning of dangers threatening its integrity. Since memory-traces can become conscious just as much as perceptions, especially through their association with verbal residues, the possibility arises of a confusion which would lead to a mistaking of reality. The ego guards itself by establishing a function for *reality-testing*, which can be allowed to fall into abeyance in dreams on account of the conditions governing the state of sleep. In its efforts to preserve itself in an environment of overwhelming mechanical forces, the ego is threatened by dangers that come in the first instance from external reality, but not from there alone. Its own id is a source of similar dangers and that for two different reasons. In the first place, an excessive strength of instinct can damage the ego in the same way as an excessive "stimulus" from the external world. It is true that such an excess cannot destroy it; but it *can* destroy its characteristic dynamic organization, it can turn the ego back into a portion of the id. In the second place, experience may have taught the ego that the satisfaction of some instinctual demand that is not in itself unbearable would involve dangers in the external world, so that an instinctual demand of that kind itself becomes a danger. Thus the ego is fighting on two fronts:

it has to defend its existence both against an external world that threatens it with annihilation and against an internal world that makes excessive demands. It adopts the same methods of protection against both, but its defense against the internal foe is particularly inadequate. As a result of having been originally identical with this enemy and of having since lived with it upon the most intimate terms, the ego has the greatest difficulty in escaping from the internal dangers. They persist as threats, even if they can be temporarily held in check.

We have heard how the weak and immature ego of the first phase of childhood is permanently damaged by the strain put upon it in the effort to ward off the dangers that are peculiar to that period of life. Children are protected against the dangers threatening them from the external world by the care of their parents; they pay for this security by a fear of losing their parents' love, which would deliver them over helpless to the dangers of the external world. This factor exercises a decisive influence upon the outcome of the conflict when a boy finds himself in the situation of the Œdipus complex and the threat aimed against his narcissism by castration, reinforced from primeval sources, takes possession of him. Driven by the combined power of these two influences, of the immediate real danger and of the remembered phylogenetic one, the child embarks upon his attempts at defense (repressions), which are effective for the moment but nevertheless turn out to be inadequate when the later reanimation of sexual life brings a reinforcement to the repudiated instinctual demands. From the biological standpoint, then, it may be said that the ego comes to grief over the task of mastering the excitations of the first sexual period, at a time when its immaturity makes it incompetent to do so. We recognize the essential precondition of neuroses in this lagging of ego development behind libidinal development; and we cannot escape the conclusion that neuroses could be avoided if the child's ego were spared this task, that is, if the child's sexual life were allowed free play, as happens among many primitive races. It may be that the etiology of neurotic illnesses is more complicated than we have here described; if so, we have at least brought into the foreground an essential part of the etiological complex. Nor should we forget the phylogenetic influences, which are present somehow in the id in forms that we are not yet able to grasp, and which must certainly operate more forcibly upon the ego during the early period that is in question than later. On the other hand we begin to perceive that such an early attempt at damming up the sexual instinct, such a decided partiality of the young ego for the external as opposed to the internal world, arising from the prohibition of infantile sexuality, cannot be without its effect upon the individual's later readiness for cultural growth. The instinctual demands, being forced aside from direct satisfaction, are compelled to take new directions which lead to substitutive satisfaction, and in the course of these *détours* they may become desexualized and their connection with their original instinctual aims may become looser. And at this point we can anticipate the idea that much of our most highly valued cultural heritage has been acquired at the cost of sexuality and by the restriction of sexual motive forces.

We have been obliged repeatedly to emphasize the fact that the ego owes its origin as well as the most important of its acquired characteristics to its relation to the real external world; and we are thus prepared to assume that the pathological states of the ego—those in which it most approximates once again to the id—are founded upon a cessation or slackening of that relation to the external world. This is in complete agreement with the clinical experience that the precipitating cause of the outbreak of a psychosis is either that reality has become intolerably painful or that the instincts have become extraordinarily intensified—both of which, in view of the rival claims made by the id and the external world upon the ego, must produce the same effect upon it. The problem of psychoses would be simple and intelligible if the withdrawal of the ego from reality could be carried through completely. But that seems rarely if ever to happen. Even in conditions so far removed from the reality of the external world as hallucinatory confusional states, one learns from patients after their recovery that at the time in some corner of their minds, as they express it, there was a normal person hidden, who watched the hubbub of the illness go past, like a disinterested spectator. I do not know if we may assume that this is so in general, but I can report the same of other psychoses with a less tempestuous course. I recollect a case of chronic paranoia in which after each attack of jealousy a dream conveyed to the analyst a correct picture of the cause, free from any trace of delusion. An interesting contrast was thus brought to light: for, while we are accustomed to discover from the dreams of neurotic patients jealousies which are alien to their waking lives, in this psychotic case the delusion which dominated the patient's daytime existence was corrected by a dream. We may probably take it as being generally true that what occurs in all such cases is a *split* in the mind. Two mental attitudes have been formed instead of a single one—one, the normal one, which takes account of reality, and another which under the influence of the instincts detaches the ego from reality. The two exist alongside each other. The issue depends upon their relative strength. If the second is or becomes the stronger, the necessary condition for a psychosis is present. If the relation is reversed, then there is an apparent cure of the delusional disorder. Actually it has only retreated into the unconscious, as indeed we are driven to conclude from numerous observations showing that a delusion has existed ready-made for a long time before its manifest outbreak.

The view which postulates that in all psychoses there is a *split in the ego* could not demand so much notice, if it were not for the fact that it turns out to apply also to other conditions more like the neuroses and, finally, to the neuroses themselves. I first convinced myself of this in cases of *fetishism*. This abnormality, which can be counted as one of the perversions, is, as is well known, based upon the patient, who is almost always male, not recognizing the fact that women have no penis—a fact which is exceedingly distasteful to him because of the evidence it affords of the possibility of his being castrated himself. He therefore rejects the perception of his own senses, which showed him that women's genitals lack a penis, and holds fast to the opposite conviction. The rejected perception, however, does not remain entirely without effects, for, in spite of everything, the patient has not the courage to assert that he really saw a penis. He snatches hold of something else instead—a part of the body or some other object—and attributes to it the rôle of the penis which he cannot do without. It is usually something that he actually saw at the moment at which he saw the woman's genitals, or it is something which can suitably serve as a symbolic substitute for the penis. Now it would not be right to describe this process which accompanies the formation of a fetish as a split in the ego; it is a compromise formed with the aid of displacement, such as we have been familiar with in dreams. But our observations show us still more. The fetish was created with the intention of destroying the evidence for the possibility of castration, so that fear of castration could be avoided. If women, like other living creatures, possess a penis, there is no need to tremble for the further possession of one's own penis. Now we come across fetishists who have developed the same dread of castration as non-fetishists and react to it in the same way. Their behavior, therefore, simultaneously expresses two contrary presuppositions. On the one hand they are denying the fact that they have perceived that women's genitals lack a penis; and on the other hand they are recognizing the fact that women have no penis and are drawing the right conclusions from it. The two attitudes persist side by side through their whole lives without affecting each other. Here is what may rightly be called a split in the ego. This circumstance also enables us to understand how it is that fetishism is so often only partially developed. It does not govern the choice of object exclusively but leaves room for a greater or lesser degree of normal sexual behavior; sometimes indeed it retires into a modest position or is limited to a mere hint. The fetishist, therefore, has never completely succeeded in detaching his ego from the reality of the external world.

It must not be thought that fetishism constitutes an exceptional case in exhibiting a split in the ego; it is merely a particularly favorable subject for study. We must return to our statement that the infantile ego, under the domination of the external world, disposes of undesirable instinctual demands by means of what are called repressions. We can now supplement this by a further assertion that, during the same period of life, the ego often enough finds itself in the position of warding off some claim from the *external world* which it feels as painful, and that this is effected by *denying* the perceptions that bring to knowledge such a demand on the part of reality. Denials of this kind often occur, and not only with fetishists; and whenever we are in a position to study them, they turn out to be half-measures, incomplete attempts at detachment from reality. The rejection is always supplemented by an acceptance; two contrary and independent attitudes always arise and this produces the fact of a split in the ego. The issue once more depends upon which of the two can command the greater intensity.

The facts concerning this split in the ego which we have just described are neither so new nor so strange as they may at first appear. It is indeed a universal characteristic of the neuroses that there are present in the subject's mental life, as regards some particular behavior, two different attitudes, contrary to each other and independent of each other; in that case, however, one of them belongs to the ego and the opposing one, which is repressed, belongs to the id. The difference between the two cases is essentially a topographical or structural one and it is not always easy to decide in the individual case with which of the two possibilities one is dealing. But they have something important in common, and it is this. Whatever defensive efforts the ego makes in warding off dangers, whether it is repudiating a portion of the external world or whether it seeks to reject an instinctual demand from the internal world, its success is never complete or unqualified; there result always two opposing attitudes, of which the defeated, weaker one, no less than the other, leads to psychological complications. Finally, it is only necessary to remark what a small proportion of all these processes become known to us through our conscious perceptions.

CHAPTER NINE

The Internal World

❧ ❧
❧ ❧

WE HAVE no way of conveying knowledge of a complicated set of simultaneous processes except by describing them successively; and thus it happens that all our accounts err in the first instance in the direction of one-sided simplification and must wait till they can be supplemented, reconstructed, and so set right.

The picture of an ego which mediates between the id and the external world, which takes over the instinctual demands of the former in order to bring them to satisfaction, which perceives things in the latter and uses them as memories, which, intent upon its self-preservation, is on guard against excessive claims from both directions, and which is governed in all its decisions by the injunctions of a modified pleasure principle—this picture actually applies to the ego only up to the end of the first period of childhood, till about the age of five. At about that time an important change has taken place. A portion of the external world has, at least partially, been given up as an object and instead, by means of identification, taken into the ego—that is, has become an integral part of the internal world. This new mental agency continues to carry on the functions which have hitherto been performed by the corresponding people in the external world: it observes the ego, gives it orders, corrects it and threatens it with punishments, exactly like the parents whose place it has taken. We call this agency the *superego* and are aware of it, in its judicial functions, as our *conscience*. It is a remarkable thing that the superego often develops a severity for which no example has been provided by the real parents, and further that it calls the ego to task not only on account of its deeds but just as much on account of its thoughts and unexecuted intentions, of which it seems to have knowledge. We are reminded that the hero of the Œdipus legend too felt guilty for his actions and punished himself, although the compulsion of the oracle should have made him innocent in our judgment and in his own. The superego is in fact the heir to the Œdipus complex and only arises after that complex has been disposed of. For that reason its excessive severity does not follow a real prototype but corresponds to the strength which is used in fending off the temptation of the Œdipus complex. Some suspicion of this state of things lies, no doubt, at the bottom of the assertion made by philosophers and believers that the moral sense is not instilled into men by education or acquired by them in the course of social life, but is implanted in them from a higher source.

So long as the ego works in complete agreement with the superego, it is not easy to distinguish between their manifestations; but tensions and estrangements between them become very plainly visible. The torments caused by the reproaches of conscience correspond precisely to a child's dread of losing his parents' love, a dread which has been replaced in him by the moral agency. On the other hand, if the ego has successfully resisted a temptation to do something that would be objectionable to the superego, it feels its self-respect raised and its pride increased, as though it had made some precious acquisition. In this way the superego continues to act the rôle of an external world toward the ego, although it has become part of the internal world. During the whole of a man's later life it represents the influence of his childhood, of the care and education given to him by his parents, of his dependence on them —of the childhood which is so greatly prolonged in human beings by a common family life. And in all of this what is operating is not only the personal qualities of these parents but also everything that produced a determining effect upon them themselves, the tastes and standards of the social class in which they live and the characteristics and traditions of the race from which they spring. Those who have a liking for generalizations and sharp distinctions may say that the external world, in which the individual finds himself exposed after being detached from his parents, represents the power of the present; that his id, with its inherited trends, represents the organic past; and that the super-ego, which comes to join them later, represents more than anything the cultural past, an after-experience of which, as it were, the child has to pass through during the few years of his early life. It is scarcely likely that such generalizations can be wholly correct. Some of the cultural acquisitions have undoubtedly left a deposit behind in the *id*; much of what is contributed by the superego will awaken an echo in the id; many of the child's new experiences will be intensified because they are repetitions of some primeval phylogenetic experience.

"Was du ererbt von deinen Vätern hast,
Erwirb es, um es zu besitzen." [14]

---

[14] [Goethe, *Faust*, Part I: "What thou hast inherited from thy fathers, acquire it to make it thine."]

Thus the superego takes up a kind of intermediate position between the id and the external world; it unites in itself the influences of the present and of the past. In the emergence of the superego we have before us, as it were, an example of the way in which the present is changed into the past. . . .

*   *   *   *   *   *   *

Index

INDEX